Reformed

Reformed

Confessions of a Preacher's Kid

Karl Petersen

RESOURCE *Publications* • Eugene, Oregon

REFORMED
Confessions of a Preacher's Kid

Copyright © 2019 Karl Petersen. All rights reserved. Except for brief quotations in critical publications or reviews, no part of this book may be reproduced in any manner without prior written permission from the publisher. Write: Permissions, Wipf and Stock Publishers, 199 W. 8th Ave., Suite 3, Eugene, OR 97401.

Resource Publications
An Imprint of Wipf and Stock Publishers
199 W. 8th Ave., Suite 3
Eugene, OR 97401

www.wipfandstock.com

PAPERBACK ISBN: 978-1-5326-7117-3
HARDCOVER ISBN: 978-1-5326-7118-0
EBOOK ISBN: 978-1-5326-7119-7

Manufactured in the U.S.A.

Contents

Preface | vii

Chapter 1: Tornado | 1

Chapter 2: Passages | 10

Chapter 3: Baptism | 17

Chapter 4: The Wandering Eye | 23

Chapter 5: Scientist Meets God | 30

Chapter 6: Abundance | 37

Chapter 7: Johnny Ball | 43

Chapter 8: Sex Education | 52

Chapter 9: Playing Church | 62

Chapter 10: The Body | 71

Chapter 11: Arthur | 77

Chapter 12: Blindsided | 85

Chapter 13: Shit | 97

Chapter 14: Canadian League | 104

Chapter 15: Aunt Jemima | 110

Chapter 16: Closing Argument | 121

Chapter 17: Splendor | 127

Chapter 18: Gargoyles | 134

Chapter 19: Crimes | 143

Chapter 20: Gathering | 152

Acknowledgements | 165

Preface

MY MOM TOLD ME I was born into darkness. The power went out at the hospital just as I was entering the world. My parents at first feared for my life and a few hours later celebrated that I'd come out more or less normal. But they maybe should have recognized my dark beginnings as fair warning of a rebellious streak in the bundle they were bringing home.

Conforming to expectations wasn't in my DNA. This might explain both the trouble I got into and my coping strategy in the Dutch subculture where I grew up. My elders proffered plenty of answers to faith and life, many of which I hold to, though their answers provoked as many questions and doubts. And the more boundaries they laid out, the more I was prone to trespass.

If you'd graced the pews of the Dutch Reformed church where my dad was pastor, you would have first noticed the singing. The Dutch are blessed with big lungs, and we could really belt out a hymn, in harmony. You might also have noticed lots of large families. Procreation was our chief method of church growth. My mom and dad, true to the call, demonstrated what they preached by producing eight of us kids.

Our church denomination was known more than anything for its preaching, cerebral and Reformed in doctrine. My dad could deliver a three-point sermon with the best of them. His sermons were clear and precise, spotless in Calvinist theology, economical in language, fenced around and parceled out as precisely as a parishioner's eighty-acre farm plot without a wasted inch of land—in every detail Dutch.

Church bored me. The songs, Dad's sermons, and the prayers seldom registered on the Richter scale of my young mind. It would be wrong to say I didn't get anything out of church, but greater than the impact of what is commonly called "church life" was the impact of the life I shared with my

PREFACE

family and community as a boy. The stories in this book are a portion of that shared life, which planted the seeds of my faith and worldview.

Many of these stories come from my family's oral history. Our stories put the "time" in supper time. Our dad could turn a phrase. I remember his cadence, dramatic pauses, wry grin, and stifled laughter. His stories begat other stories around the table, which begat still more stories in a long line of begats down through the years. We could consume an entire evening with tales about each other, about who did what and when, all sufficiently redacted and amplified in their successive retellings.

These events took place in my formative childhood years in the 1960's. For the most part, the political turbulence of the time was background noise to me—Martin Luther King, the Kennedys, Vietnam, the hippy movement. We were somewhat insulated from the broad American landscape by the fact of our immigrant culture and religious faith, which emphasized our distinctiveness from the world that lay outside. You might say we were even more exceptional than the America we lived in. We had a saying, "If you ain't Dutch, you ain't much." I would add that if you weren't Reformed, you were misinformed.

The subtitle, *Confessions of a Preacher's Kid*, is not entirely tongue in cheek. Being a preacher's kid came with expectations that posed a difficult burden in a community with a rigorous code of conduct. My peers held a common conviction that I should stand out as an example of upright behavior on account of my dad's title. If anything else, this book should confirm my parents' belief that a preacher's kid is no better than anyone else and stands equally in need of (if not more in need of) the grace of God.

A book of stories looking back fifty years admittedly presents some difficulties, the most obvious being the question of accuracy. Our human inclination is to want the undisputed facts, as from an objective news report or court of law, but this puts unrealistic demands on us. Most people's minds don't work like video recorders. Our memories usually serve us pea soup rather than peas. We are event shapers, stirring the pot, blending, tasting, stirring again, and trying to make sense of it all. Our stories say, "Here, take a sip and see if that's about right." And in the end, most of us would agree the pea soup is far more satisfying, perhaps even more truthful, than the hard facts of uncooked peas, especially after adding the herbs and spices, and the ham . . . oh, the ham!

That said, I am confident I've got the right ingredients here. The events in these stories actually happened, and the places and people in them are

PREFACE

real, while the names of some characters have been changed. Where I am off in substance, I apologize in advance and welcome challengers for their recollections. I'm confident that others' versions of events would simply add more ingredients to a wonderful blend. On my side, let it be known, the statute of limitations for my crimes of yore has long passed.

The unreliability of memory aside, the distance of years offers one great advantage, namely, perspective. In our youth we simply live moments as they happen. Only when we look back with the light of time, do we better understand why some events seem to stay so firmly lodged in our memories, while others are lost. As we draw lines between the dots, we uncover themes we may not have noticed before. And mysteriously, we may find our stories are not only uniquely personal but also universal, bonding us with each other in a common timeless narrative. My hope is that my readers find this to be true as they read these stories.

My parents possessed the same plain-spoken simplicity of the people they served, and I have tried to reflect that simplicity here in my writing, honoring the characters and the oral tradition that has faithfully carried these memories this far. This book is dedicated to the community of my childhood, my parents, and my siblings, all of whom for better or worse bear some responsibility for who I am.

Vancouver
January, 2019

www.karlpetersen.com

Chapter 1

Tornado

I REMEMBER THE SOUND LIKE a freight train in the hollow air. I remember panic, words shouted, intoned, and prayed into the basement ceiling, the dank smell of the concrete walls. Most of all, I remember the images—the green clouds, ice balls, the cellar door, feet on wooden stairs, and pigs stuck in mud.

It was a balmy day, May 1962 in Platte, South Dakota. In the backyard hailstones were pelting down like white marbles. After the marbles came golf balls, followed minutes later by baseballs, homeruns flying over the backyard fence and bouncing thunderously off the ground. Some people later claimed they had them the size of softballs at their place.

Mom never did well with dangerous weather, unfortunately, because South Dakota had plenty of it. My oldest sister, Sharon, was Mom's biggest support after Dad, but she was off to college, and Dad was away at a pastors' conference in Michigan. That left my teenage brothers, Don and Dale, in charge of helping Mom watch the rest of us. At the moment, Don and Dale were running all over the backyard, gathering ice balls as they thudded to the ground. They made a game to see who could find the largest one without getting knocked out as the hail grew in size.

Mom screamed at them through the screen door to get inside, but it was no use. I was only six, but if my sister Nancy hadn't had a grip on me, I would've run out to join them.

Don and Dale finally came jostling into the kitchen with baseball mitts full of trophy hailstones and laid them out on the table to compare. My little brother Ken and I gazed at eye level while Nancy held Keith up so he could see.

"Ice!" Shirley yelled.

We all leaned in with stunned amazement over the bulbous pile as though presented with a newborn baby. I picked up one hailstone and held it reverently. The cold stung my hands. To think it had been tossed up and down by air currents, conceived and grown thousands of feet in the stratosphere, and now this ice ball had visited our home like a strange guest from another country. Then I started to cry as I noticed the ice melting and running over the Formica table top.

"The hailstones are dying!"

Quickly choosing the largest hailstones, we stuffed them into the freezer to show Dad when he got home because he would never believe it otherwise.

Even as we celebrated, it appeared the sky was not finished releasing her load. The hail came with even greater ferocity. Mom turned away, but the seven of us kids—Don, Dale, Nancy, Shirley, me, Ken, and Keith—watched out the back windows to the west like spectators at a live museum. A heavy darkness was gathering, portending calamity.

"I wish your dad was home." Mom sighed. "What terrible timing. Just like with that fire. Wouldya ever!" It was her favorite expression—wouldya ever—an unfinished question that captured the confounding mystery of the moment.

The hail storm ended as quickly as it had begun, leaving a surreal landscape of ice balls strewn across the yard. Dark green-tinged clouds were roiling and billowing like malignant tumors, dwarfing the grove on the far side of the church parking lot.

We had had the radio on the whole afternoon because they were announcing a "tornado watch," which simply meant the sky was ripe with potential, so "heads up." Tornado watches were standard in this weather, like the kind of good advice you might get not to go near a sow with a litter. But that afternoon the "watch" turned to a "warning," which meant a funnel cloud had touched down west of town.

An eerie quiet had settled in over the town. In the stillness, we could make out a low roar, an unmistakable rumbling, like a freight train approaching its next station. The quiet was suddenly penetrated by the siren blaring from the Platte water tower.

Don was standing in the parking lot for a clearer view of the oncoming weather but turned and ran toward the house, where he found Dale gaping skyward, transfixed by the mass of clouds churning with earth and debris and half of Platte Lake it seemed. Don screamed for him to get in the house.

"Tornado!" Don yelled as he and Dale rushed into the kitchen. "Everybody! Down in the basement!"

We knew the drill, tip-tapping single file down the wooden steps to the damp concrete-walled basement. Even two-year-old Keith toddled down with purpose in his step. We stood huddled in the basement's southwest corner, refugees in our own house.

Don and Dale quickly counted to make sure we were all there . . . seven.

"We've only got seven!" Dale yelled. "Who's missing?"

"Dad and Sharon," Nancy announced.

"No! Besides them! Somebody's not here!"

We looked around. All of us were accounted for.

"Mom!" somebody yelled. "Where's Mom?"

Don was at the top of the stairs in three leaps, screaming for Mom. We could hear his footsteps back and forth over the floor of our large two-story house. Two minutes later, they appeared at the top of the basement steps, Mom first, followed by Don. We were a mix of relief and confusion.

"Where were you?" we all wanted to know.

"I was sitting out on the front porch watching the storm and singing," she explained, as matter-of-factly as if waiting for bread to bake.

The front porch was a favorite evening nook, large and screened in, flanked by mature elm trees, offering the perfect spot on a quiet spring night. But this evening was not quiet, and the front porch was not the right spot to be watching the storm because it was at the end of the house opposite the approaching tornado. It would have struck before she'd known what hit her. Was it a moment of absent-mindedness . . . or was she lost in the thought of what it would be like to be swept away from the overwhelming responsibility of watching over a brood of eight kids, all with minds of their own? Who could have blamed her?

"Oh well, forget about it," Mom said, trying to minimize the urgency of the moment. "We're all down here now safe and sound, so let's not fret." And then she added quietly, "I wish your dad was here." She pulled her sweater more tightly around her. "Just like the fire."

"Mom," Nancy said, "the fire was way downtown."

"Yeah, but it was big. What if that had reached us?"

The siren continued to howl, meaning we could still be in the path of the tornado. We wouldn't know until it either hit us or the siren stopped. I wondered if we'd be plucked from the earth like Dorothy in *The Wizard of*

Oz with our whole house spinning into the sky. Would we go on Dorothy's perilous ride to that creepy psychedelic place of munchkins, witches, and flying monkeys?

I looked up to the basement ceiling, the underside of what had been solid footing since my first steps. And beyond that, the siren wailed, starting low and rising, to what some claimed was an A flat, for ten seconds before slowly descending several octaves to a moan.

The town first got the siren during World War Two when someone had worried about bombing raids, which obviously never happened. Later the town kept the siren as a warning against a nuclear attack, which also never happened. Nevertheless, it proved useful for fires, tornados, and lunch time. It became a constant companion, whistling in danger and whistling for lunch. The whistle, as we came to call it, went off daily at twelve o'clock, meaning lunch, a reminder every noon to drop everything. A crowbar clanged to the floor of the shop, a pen dropped to the ledger, and one more clothespin was clasped to the line of wash with a glance to the sky. It was that most sacred of hours—lunch hour.

The whistle was a constant message that there were more important things in life than hard work—there was someone to share a laugh with over a thermos of soup and a sandwich, to hear your jokes or sob stories for the umpteenth time and laugh or cry as if hearing your story for the first time. Those few seconds from the whistle's high whine down to a fading drone was a daily recital of the town's perennial story of success and disappointment, hope and betrayal. On a clear day the farmers for miles around heard it and remembered good harvests as the whistle ascended and harvests that fell short as the whistle faded. It was a reminder not to get too cocky about the day's fortunes because tomorrow it could all be lost in a moment—a call to both gratitude and reverence.

"Thy will be done," Mom murmured quietly, fumbling with a Kleenex tissue as we waited. "Just pray," she said. "God will protect us. If the tornado comes, we'll still be with Him, here or there."

There was no arguing that. "Here or there" is what tornados did, jumping here or there, on this house or that, keeping you on this earth or sending you to your maker. Tornados were the great dividers. I imagined us whirling around in the funnel cloud, passing each other, reaching out a hand to grab on to the next person.

"Why doesn't God just make the tornado go away?" I asked.

No one answered. God may be great, I thought, but there were some things even bigger than he was, like tornadoes, and he could do nothing about it.

Mom took a deep breath. I thought she was about to start singing "When Peace Like a River" again when she suddenly stepped over to the fruit cellar. The cellar was an alcove off the main basement with an arched concrete ceiling and stairs that led outside through an overhead door of wood slats, a thin barrier between us and whatever waited outside. You would only have to push it upward to find out what was there.

"Where you going, Mom?" someone asked.

"Just want to grab some of this fruit."

Dale followed her, made sure the cellar door was latched, and pulled Mom back, her arms bulging with canned fruit to be put in a safer place. The cellar door rattled lightly. Whatever price we had to pay, she figured her hard work would not go to waste on a tornado.

That morning, I had been sitting outside on that same door, drawing in the dirt with a stick, listening to the cicadas and the breeze whispering in the giant elms like a mother to her child. It was the sound of home, comfort, and deep-down grounding, unlike any other prayer. But in a few hours those whispers had been replaced by the low thrumming of impending violence.

After a few more minutes, someone thought the rumbling of the tornado was growing softer. We would have been mistaken to assume the tornado had turned course because tornadoes had minds of their own. They were drunken, meandering forces, veering unpredictably left or right, pausing momentarily, or speeding ahead. They could start as harmless funnel clouds that never actually touched down and suddenly become wide swaths of cyclonic power spinning at 250 miles per hour.

Some of the townspeople felt it foolish to pray the prayer that no tornadoes would come their way because, they argued, tornados were simply a part of prairie life. You took yours if and when it came. It was unfair to ask God to send a tornado elsewhere, which would by elimination simply mean another town or farm rather than your own would be hit. The one always paid the price for the many, so you'd best always be prepared for your time to pay. Glancing up at the basement ceiling, we prayed that the house would pay the price for us by being taken up and leaving us behind, unharmed.

"Mom," I said, "I have to go pee."

"You can't go upstairs," Don said.

"But I have to go."

"Just squeeze it."

"Pee down the drain," someone suggested.

Before anyone could disagree, I was already aiming for the drain in the basement floor. My little brother Ken suddenly had to pee as well, and we played sword fights with our criss-crossing yellow streams.

The air outside had grown quiet. Don told everyone to stay put while he went to the cellar door and pushed it up just enough to peek outside. A silver streak of light reached in from the west, piercing the basement's dark interior.

"I don't think we should go out yet, Don," Mom said.

"I'm just gonna check it out."

We emerged, following Don, like remnant creatures of the earth through the cellar door. The tornado appeared to have gone. A few branches had fallen, but all around nothing else appeared to have been touched.

The next thing we knew, Don took off running as if going to grab the tornado by the tail before it got away. He raced across the street to Max's Machine Shop, his Brownie camera in hand, and was climbing onto the shop roof for a better look. He had to know what was going on. Everything needed to be documented, he figured, to go with his account of the storm. He loved weather of all kinds, the more dramatic the better, even grumbling if there hadn't been a blizzard or tornado of late. And now he was determined to enjoy the full course he'd unwittingly ordered up with his laments and prayers. He stood on the roof peak of the machine shop snapping pictures, silhouetted against the dark clouds and distant flashes of lightning as he panned back and forth with his camera like a human weathervane.

A few long minutes later, he came back with a report, which he shared with us at length, more like a preacher than a weatherman, demonstrating with grand gestures the tornado's wonder, fury, and wrath.

"It was huge, really wide. I witnessed it. It took out the farm across the road, and I watched it go right around town. The funnel cloud was thick black, and it had brown and green stuff swirling around in it, circling around and around in the tornado." He showed us with wide gyrations of his hips. He was enraptured, one with the tornado, possessed by it. His body twisted and contorted until he *was* the tornado.

"Yeah, Don, do the twist!" Shirley yelled, mimicking him.

"The tail was wagging back and forth like this," Don said, wagging his backside.

"Like a dog?" Shirley asked.

"I filled up a whole roll of film. Man!" He paused to take a breath before continuing his inspirational message for another five or ten minutes.

The reports on the radio confirmed our fire and brimstone preacher had delivered the truth. It was an F4 tornado. The wind speeds were strong enough to level a well-constructed house, to toss cars like toys, and to throw things through the air like missiles. The tornado had turned north just as it reached Platte, enigmatically skirting the town limits before it again veered northeast. Lots of property was lost from surrounding farms, but so far, it was reported, human life had been spared.

It was a miracle announced in the papers, preached from the Sunday pulpits, and talked about in every kitchen and diner at the noon whistle from Platte to towns fifty miles away. In church the next Sunday we would sing hymns affirming God was our shield and ever-present help in times of trouble. But the obvious questions about a selective mercy that allowed other people to lose their homes while ours was spared had not yet prodded my young mind.

Tornados leave a vacuum filled with awe. But whatever reverence we felt must have been lost the day after the tornado because all of us, moved by some perverse desire to observe the wanton destruction wrecked upon the land, loaded into the Rambler station wagon to have a look around.

The tornado was a scythe that had cut a large swath through farmland to the west before zigzagging north. We pulled over to the side of the road, where several other cars were parked in a long line. We gaped at holes left by a farm and farmhouse that were no longer there. They had been ripped from their moorings and scattered like pick up sticks across an adjacent field. A door lay flat on the ground like an entryway to the underworld. A tractor and a plow were the only items that remained untouched.

"Where are the people?" I asked apprehensively.

"There was nobody here," Don said. "The people sold the place and the new people weren't moved in yet."

"Are they gonna make a new house?"

At the edge of a hole that was a basement, a few gawkers stood looking in as if at an open grave. There were a few words of sadness and condolences mumbled to the ground as people kicked things aside to see what they could find. Strewn across the ground lay questions one could only speculate the answers to. Someone picked up a picture of the Badlands and said, "Isn't that ironic?"

I spotted something red in the debris and grabbed it—a Tonka truck, rusted out, missing a wheel. I turned to Mom to ask if I could keep it, but before I'd uttered the first word, Mom said, "No, you can't have that. Put it down."

"But Mom, the people left it."

"But it's not ours. Put it down, now."

I dropped it and stared, thinking it would do no one any good just left there, and imagined what good I could make of it. When we got back to the car, Mom explained that it was important to respect those who had lost so much.

"But if they died, they won't care if I have it because they can't play with it anymore."

"It doesn't matter," Mom said firmly, and that was the end of it. For Mom, certain assumptions of behavior prevailed even against the common sense of a six-year-old.

We drove on to Pfeifer's pig farm. The word was the tornado had missed the Pfeifer house by only a few feet. If you learned anything from a tornado, it was that life and death were mere inches apart. When we arrived, Terry Pfeifer was standing in the yard between the house and barn engaged in a good jaw flapping with his neighbor lady to the north.

"Hey Terry!" Don said as we piled out.

"Edith here got took up by the tornado!" Terry announced.

Without missing a beat, Edith continued her story, as she tried to catch her breath. "So as soon as we're done with supper, Henry leans back in his chair and says, how about some of those peaches for dessert? I said, those are gone, I'll have to go to the cellar and get some more. So I go outside and as I'm opening the cellar door, I look up and it looks like we might be getting a bad thunderstorm. But we never heard nothing about a tornado. Shoulda had the radio on, I guess. So I grab a fresh jar of peaches, and I'm coming back up out of the cellar, and that's the last thing I remember before I'm lying in the middle of the field about fifty yards from the house! The tornado musta sucked me right out of the cellar, I don't know. Anyway, I look over to my left and there's Henry sitting right there with his spoon still in his fist like he's waiting for some peaches! He broke his arm, but the spoon's just fine. On top of that, we managed to find a jar of peaches perfectly untouched." She had us laughing.

Terry led our tribe out behind his barn to a pasture where he kept his pigs. We came to a hollow with a mud hole near the bottom of it where his pigs would wallow. His pigs were all there, lying stone still where the tornado had slammed them into the mud. It was like a battlefield scattered with wounded and dead hogs. We walked among them, checking for signs of life. Near the pond a couple of pigs were stuck neck deep, unable to move. They simply grunted a couple of mournful, lonely grunts as if to say, "No rush, but when you have a minute . . . "

"What are you going to do with them all?" Don asked.

"Help me out here," Terry said.

They turned a couple over.

"Not a scratch on them," Terry said. "I say too good to waste and good enough to eat."

He said he'd send them to get butchered, but the word would come back later that they were no good. The meat from every pig was shot through with shards of wood. They'd died a gruesome death.

As we drove home, scattered debris on the ground flashed by the car window as if still caught in the tornado—tree branches, barn siding, a chair, t-shirts, a Cubs baseball cap. The word was no one had been seriously injured and not one soul was lost. Like Jesus sending demons into the swine, somebody said, God had let the pigs take the hit for us. No souls were lost, but in a way I couldn't have explained, mine was somehow found when that funnel cloud touched down. God had got my attention.

—— Chapter 2 ——

Passages

Platte Lake could always take the edge off a hot summer day. I was seven, in my new swim suit, when I saw an inner tube nearby floating free. I put it around my waist and bounced off the sandy lake bottom, feeling safe enough to go out over my head. Before I got very far, a kid stepped toward me.

"Is that yours?" he asked. "I doubt it very much because it's mine."

He grabbed at the inner tube, and I let it go without argument. He was obviously not from around here. The locals knew that toys were shared the same way the lake was shared, and if you took something, you simply left it where you found it when you were done with it.

I tiptoed from shore without the inner tube into slightly deeper water, feeling confident in my new red plaid swimming trunks. I went out up to my neck and reached out one more step, but my foot did not find bottom. I was instantly in over my head. I paddled furiously, trying to break the surface, but for some reason I couldn't. In a panic, I sucked in a mouthful of water. The sounds from outside—dads cheering their kids, girls screaming gleefully—turned muffled as from a distant world. Suddenly, I felt a hand out of nowhere grab me and lift me out of the water in a long arch through the air into shallower water. I coughed up water until I'd recovered enough to turn and look for the person who'd rescued me. No one was there.

I walked wet to the picnic tables, where my family was packing up our supplies to leave. I stood for a moment, shivering. I was too frightened to tell anyone what had happened because speaking it might cause it to happen again, and who would believe a story about the invisible hands that had saved me. A cicada hummed somewhere in the canopy of trees, a sound I associated with the comfort of home, reminding me that I was on dry land and still alive.

"Cold?" Dad asked, seeing me shiver. He wrapped me in a towel.

"Yeah," I said, but I wasn't. I was just scared.

A few minutes later, we were about to leave when an ambulance rushed into the parking lot, and two medics ran down to the beach. I ran after them. There were rumblings that some guy had just been pulled out of the lake.

I saw a crowd of white legs standing like cattails at the shore. Among them lay a large still body covered with a blanket. The medic pulled back the cover, and I could see his face. His mouth hung gaping, his lips blue, his face ashen. So this is what death looked like, what I might look like if not for those strong hands. Was it him? I stared, imagining myself lying there.

To me it was obvious. The way of water was like the way of tornados—some saved, some not. I felt my turn was just around the corner to be one of the "not saved." I had nightmares about drowning. Finally, I told my dad that I was afraid I was going to drown.

"You're not going to drown," he said. "We'll take care of you."

But I *had* almost drowned, I thought, and you weren't there. And who was taking care of that man who did drown? That guy's dad was not there, either, and there were no invisible hands to pull him to safety. Mom prayed with me my standard bedtime prayer to try to help me fall asleep, "Now I lay me down to sleep . . . ," but I stopped at "if I should die before I wake" because that was exactly what I was afraid of, that big "if." I can't remember ever swimming in Platte Lake again after that.

Fears of drowning were put at bay, for a time, when a big moment in our family happened the following spring. Dad announced we were moving to the far side of the country. I lay on my stomach on our faded brown living room carpet. My elbows propped open a map book with the sun angling low through the high sash windows.

"Where's Sumas?" I asked Dad.

The atlas showed the forty-eight contiguous states, each state in a different color. The country looked like a fantasyland made up of a vibrant patchwork of bright colors. There were pictures printed on the various states to show distinguishing features of each area. Next to New York was a picture of the Statue of Liberty, by Pittsburgh a steel factory, by St. Louis an arch called "Gateway to the West."

"Do we get to go through this arch," I asked.

"No, this way." Dad's finger glided over the page from South Dakota westward through Wyoming and Montana over mountains to the far upper left portion of the map, where the state of Washington sat in green. Its peninsula dangled over the Pacific like a hooked flounder unable to shake loose.

"Sumas is right about here by this apple. That's what Washington's famous for."

Apples? That didn't sound as interesting as the Mickey Mouse that was emblazoned on southern California. Why couldn't we move there?

"It's way in the corner," I said, disappointed. This Sumas we were headed to felt remote and alone. "Look, it's almost in Canada!"

"Almost, it's right on the border. You could probably walk into Canada from our house."

"Would they let us?"

"You have to ask first before you cross."

"What's Sumas like?" I asked dubiously.

"They have a nice school, just like the one here. Lots of kids to play ball with. I can't wait to try one of those apples, yum, yum!" he said dramatically, trying to give our future new home a positive spin though he didn't seem to know much more about it than I did.

The previous day at supper, Dad had told us that he "got a call" to serve the church in Sumas. The announcement brought us all up straight, the way it did every time one of these announcements came. We wanted to know about the school, what kids did for fun, whether the new house had a basketball hoop. Dad said he and Mom had talked about it but wanted to run the idea by the whole family because he believed, as always, that we should all be included in the decision. But I could tell he'd already made up his mind. This was more than a phone call. It was a call from God and, in the end, not really up for debate.

As I lay on the living room floor, Dad looking over my shoulder, I turned in the atlas to the full map of Washington State, nearly the last page, almost forgotten in the "W's".

"It says about Sumas—population 629," I said, reading in the margin. "Is that bigger or smaller than Platte?"

"About the same . . . a little smaller. When we get there, they'll have to change their population sign to 639," Dad smirked. I checked his face and he laughed.

Dad's mood, the colorful map, and my love for discovering new places dispelled my apprehensions, for the moment, about leaving Platte for a new home halfway across the continent. In my eight-year-old mind it would be like going on a family vacation. This would be a cinch.

One April afternoon in 1964, the American Van Lines truck pulled up in front of our house. Dad was impressed that the new church agreed to pay for our moving expenses. I stood in awe of the size of the moving truck. After we left by car, the plan was for the movers to empty our house and load the truck, and after driving non-stop, they would have all our stuff in our new house two thousand miles away in advance of our arrival. For us, it would be three long days of driving with two motel stays. Mom was glad we didn't have to do anything about moving our things. She didn't want to empty our home of eleven years, which had seen our family increase from seven to ten, and see it suddenly bare of life.

Early the next morning, still rubbing the sleep from our eyes, we piled into our Rambler station wagon and set off—Mom, Dad, and five of us eight kids. Sharon, the oldest, was finishing up her college term in Michigan. Don and Dale would finish their year of high school and follow on their own later.

My world to that point in time with all its familiar details disappeared in minutes behind us—our old two-story house; the sack swing in our back yard; the fence with the looping crest fringe; the towering elms; the wooden cellar door; the church, where I'd sat restlessly twice every Sunday counting the peppermints in my pocket; the gravel parking lot, where I'd learned to ride my green Schwinn bike; and beyond that the small grove. As we passed the last row of houses of Platte, we went through vast seas of corn and wheat, which had taught me the meaning of infinity. Near Platte Lake, Mom told us to wave goodbye because we wouldn't be seeing it anymore, but I didn't wave. I wanted to put behind me the fear it had caused me.

The landscape and its life-shaping memories, was all history in the time it took to disappear through the rear window of our station wagon. The six people in the car with me were my only landscape now. Paul Harvey, America's ubiquitous news man, came on the radio. No matter the time zone, he was on at twelve noon every day. Dad turned up the volume, anticipating Harvey's folksy, resonate voice. "Hello Americans, this is Paul Harvey. Stand by for *news*!" He was a loose tendril from home that we could hold on to until the land we came to next would lay hold of our roots.

A lot of things were happening around the time of our move. The Beatles were always on the radio, but Mom couldn't listen to "that junk" when we could be listening to the Bill Gaither Trio. She would turn the dial until she found "a decent station." For Mom, "I Wanna Hold Your Hand" had nothing over "He Touched Me." Also that year, the first Gemini spacecraft was launched, and the first Ford Mustang came off the assembly line, sparkling white. The world felt full of possibilities. And Dad was feeling enough optimism to take us clear across the country in our copper-toned Rambler sedan rather than in one of those new Mustangs. I looked out into the blue prairie sky, thinking I might spot the Gemini.

    We stopped one last time at Wall Drug, a roadside tourist trap with wall to wall old west paraphernalia—buffalo heads, spurs, mechanical horses, jackalopes, and cowboy humor. We got some postcards to send to friends back home, which Mom thought might help us with the leaving process. One postcard had a picture of a cowboy being bucked off his horse and flying through the air. The caption said, "Trust in God, cuz right about now it's all you've got." We kept that one as a souvenir. It sounded made for the moment.

    We slept, read, and did the alphabet, naming things we saw on the highway. When Dad felt we were getting a little too nostalgic about what we'd left behind, he suddenly shouted, "Hey!"

    Our heads pivoted and strained to see what he was looking at—nothing but vast stretches of rolling hills in every direction.

    "Hey what, Dad?"

    "Right there," he said to a chorus of groans as he pointed to bales of hay dotting the hillside.

    "That's your *H*, do you have an *H* yet?"

    "We're way past *H*! We're on *P* and there's nothing around but hay!"

    "*P* . . . Petersens!" Dad offered.

    Beyond Deadwood, South Dakota, tumbleweeds clung to fence lines as we wound through an eerie landscape of rust-red hills without a soul or building in sight.

    "Why— why—WHY—?" Dad said.

        "Why what?" Everyone looked up.

    "—oming. Wyoming. That sign says we're in Wyoming," he joked, trying to keep our spirits up but then laughed at our lack of amusement. Then he'd try something else. He had us guess the mileage from our location to a spot where the highway crested a hill in the distance, and after the suspenseful arrival at the marked spot, he checked the odometer and declared the winner. Then it started over again as he marked the next point where the highway disappeared on the skyline. We burned off a good part of the afternoon that way, and before we knew it, we were well into Montana.

It was late afternoon. We were near "Custer's last stand," where Custer and his cavalry were wiped out by Crazy Horse. It was forbidding territory, barren with deep gullies. My fascination with war made me want to see where "Yellow Hair" and his men had got scalped. Dad said we didn't have time. We had to find a motel soon, so he told us the story of Custer's Last Stand, making Custer sound like a hero, right up there with Davy Crockett. Something told me Custer must have been pretty stupid though to go up against thousands of Indians with only 300 men.

We stayed overnight at a motel, blanketed by wide open skies and the smell of sage. The next day we approached a pass in the Rocky Mountains. Large flakes of snow were coming down and quickly melted after hitting the windshield in little splats. Two locals wearing John Deere caps passed us in a pickup, spraying up slush. They honked and pointed at our car. We gawked as one multi-headed creature crammed into our Rambler, and they gawked back.

"Why were they pointing at our car?" I asked. I thought they were laughing at us, telling us to go home where we came from, but Dad figured something must be up and stopped to check the car. Underneath, a thin stream of gas trickled down from a hole in the gas tank. It had been punctured by a rock we'd kicked up from the road.

We took the opportunity to get out and stretch and held out our hands to catch the snow. The high altitude air smelled cold and metallic. We were shrouded in clouds and couldn't see far. Distances and height were impossible to measure. I felt we must be at the highest place on earth in the otherworldly unknown, enveloped by a snow-saturated sky.

I wondered if my parents really knew what they were doing bringing us out here, a bunch of flatlanders into the Rocky Mountains in our pathetic little Rambler with a punctured gas tank. Dad waved to passing vehicles for help until a very familiar looking semi pulled over, an American Van Lines moving truck. It was the very one that held all our earthly belongings.

"Wouldya ever," Mom chuckled to herself.

Together with Dad, the movers hemmed and hawed about what to do with the punctured gas tank, looking around into the sky as if the answer lay up there somewhere. Then Dad suggested quietly, "How about a wad of gum? Will that work?"

One of the movers shrugged, chewed up a couple of sticks of Juicy Fruit, and slid under our car. He came out a minute later giggling to himself.

"That plugged it," he said. "Seems to be holding for now."

There was nothing else to do but get to a service station as soon as possible. We pulled into the nearest town, left our car at a repair shop, got a motel room, and the next day we were on the road again with the hole welded shut.

"See, God is taking care of us," Mom said over her shoulder to us and then at Dad. "Isn't that just the thing?"

Dad was trying to read the road signs half caked with snow. "What's that?" he said, checking his watch.

"The way God provided," Mom said. "I mean, a wad of bubble gum!"

"Yep, that's true," Dad said with a sigh, his hand going over his bald top, wondering what other contingencies lay ahead.

The radio had nothing but sound-dust across the dial. Mom started in singing "Blessed Assurance," tears rolling down her cheeks as the Rambler with its seven pilgrims wound down out of the Rockies.

The weather was clearing, and we finally got a look at the mountains in all their massive splendor. Mom was in ecstasy. "Isn't it grand!" she exclaimed, waving a hand toward the same mountains that had nearly had us trapped in their capricious power.

We passed through the Idaho panhandle into Washington State with one more mountain range to cross—the Cascades—which went without incident as it started to rain. Somewhere, down these mountains in the gathering dark, between the Cascade Range and the inlets of the Pacific Ocean, lay our new home. It wouldn't be long now, but it was so foreign I wasn't sure anymore that I wanted to go there.

— Chapter 3 —

Baptism

WE PULLED INTO THE gravel driveway at the end of our three day trip to Sumas. It was night, and it was raining, but through the darkness we could make out a more modern, ranch style house, which Dad had so eagerly anticipated. Compared to our two-story home in Platte, it felt small and squashed down under a heavy sky. Inside, we were amazed to find our belongings piled high throughout the house. Mom cracked open boxes and turned circles while she wondered where things were. Our beds were all set up already in their assigned rooms, and familiar beds were all that mattered at the moment. Keith, Ken, and I went to sleep without protest in our shared room.

The next morning, I gazed up from my lower bunk to the underside of Ken's, the top bunk, which was his because he was younger and lighter. Rain was still coming down. It sounded torrential on the corrugated fiberglass cover over the breezeway between the house and garage. I imagined water rising to engulf me before Ken, three feet higher, even knew what was happening.

"Ken, you awake?"

He didn't answer. From across the room came Keith's faint snoring. The first morning in Sumas I was alone in my thoughts. The rain slowed to a whisper down the gutters like the lines of a new story.

We would have to learn the ways of the rain here, how it could come on so cunningly, like a silver-tongued salesman with something up its sleeve, clouds brooding awhile until finally closing with an unrelenting babble, then calming to a murmur, then prattling on with an overstated sales pitch, ignoring our pleadings that it was time to shut it down and move on.

The rain in Platte, on the other hand, came down like a beefy handshake—frank and all-present. What you saw was what you got. The clouds would roll in over the plains like a neighbor with purpose in his stride, linger at your house an hour over coffee, and finally settle his business before moving on. Then the sun would come out more brilliantly for having cleared the air. But here, no one was sure when the rain started or when it would leave. It just always seemed to be there, knocking.

I got out of bed and wandered into the hall, not sure which way to turn in my new home. The house was silent. Beyond the boxes in the living room, I found the big picture window that looked out to Mt. Baker, which I could still not see for the clouds. Grass poked up above shallow pools covering the lawn. The ground here did not lap up the rain like a parched dog as it did on the prairies. I sat over a vent throwing out warm air, tucked my knees under my chin, and brushed my hand over the plush carpet.

Dad walked us to school the first day. Nancy was in seventh grade, I was in third, and Ken in first. Keith was four and not in school yet, and Shirley would be going off to boarding school soon a hundred and fifty miles south. Our new school was alive with enthusiasm. As I bit into my peanut butter and jelly sandwich, I heard kids shouting on the playground, marching and chanting something about wanting "old water." I couldn't understand why they'd be complaining about the water when this place had enough fresh water for thousands of Sumases. Then I realized they were chanting a political slogan—"Goldwater, Goldwater, he's our man! Johnson belongs in the garbage can!" I hadn't even heard of Goldwater, but the political climate was intense. Goldwater (Republican) was running against Johnson (Democrat) for president in 1964, and Goldwater had convinced folks here that the Republican Party was "the farmers' party" and he was the only thing standing between them and Johnson taking over their farms. Kids were parroting the voices of their parents with their pro-Goldwater march. It was a catchy jingle, I thought, especially the reference to putting someone in the garbage can, so I joined in.

Dad assured us there was nothing to worry about, that the church and the people were very much like those in Platte. "Same kind of people, in a different place," he said. "It'll take some getting used to."

But I didn't know if I wanted to get used to it. I cried at my desk during class. It was all too foreign. What had initially taken shape in my mind as a trip to the West Coast on a glorified vacation had hardened into the realization of permanent separation from the place and friends I knew. The new classroom was an unknown kingdom with bland décor and odd requirements, loud voices, impossible tasks, and a teacher who didn't seem to care much for her job. She got noticeably irritated with my sobbing and chastised me, which only made me cry more. How was she to know how depression could infect a kid jolted out of his home and transported thousands of miles away to a strange land? At her wit's end, she finally assigned Neil Kamphouse, a classmate, to be my friend and protector to make sure I got a fair chance on the baseball diamond and in all games. Neil was the first to show me personal kindness, and he was a leader in the class, so our association elevated my status. Neil took on his assignment with creative zeal by arranging fights between me and kids he thought were picking on me to give me a chance to show I belonged. I won a couple times, but it was not enough to dispel the gray haze in my head.

Meanwhile, the rain continued. The dampness infused everything, creeping through the walls, through bed sheets, through shoes and clothes, right to the bone until it made you squeak. The water table was so high the crawl space under our house had standing water constantly during the winter rains. It was no wonder no one had basements. We complained to each other with sarcastic names for our new home like "Chance of Rain Washington," "Wash a ton," or "Always Washing Washington." Mom would come back with, "If it wasn't for the rain, we wouldn't enjoy the lush, green beauty either, so let's not fret and just take what God gives us."

In spite of Mom's beseeching us towards gratefulness, the dampness was the thorn in her own flesh. She had sinus problems. Along with the incessant drip of rain came the draining of her nose into facial tissues. Her sentences were often fragmented by a barrage of fierce nose blowing. She could never leave the house without a mittful of Kleenex in her purse, and then when the sniffles started and she opened her purse, it exploded in a white furry.

Over the years, we would learn to live not only *with* the water but *in* it, playing outside with rain running down our faces as though it were sunshine on the prairies. Football games in the rain on a soggy patch of ground and sliding until our clothes were indistinguishable from the muddy turf became a favorite pastime. Umbrellas were considered an unnecessary burden. No one used them.

And we learned to enjoy camping in all weather. Dad discovered the marvels of tent trailers one summer and bought one, a Sears special, cheap and practical, that he said was good enough to keep the rain out. Since tent trailers could only sleep four, Dad also took the extra zip-on room at a reduced rate to accommodate all of us. But Sears could not compete with the ubiquitous rain. Puddles formed at night on the canvas roof of the extra room, where Ken and I slept on cots. The rain seeped through in large drips, then in a steady trickle, and down into the cotton batting of our sleeping bags onto raw skin. Dad woke up periodically to push up on the roof to slough off the rain, but it wasn't enough. By morning the rain had stopped as we peeled ourselves out of wet bags.

"It's a little sloppy this morning," Dad announced through the tent flap and added to keep up our morale, "but it smells nice and fresh when you get out of the tent."

We stepped around puddles and shivered as we sipped hot cocoa and ate oatmeal smothered in brown sugar.

Dale and Don joined us in Sumas after finishing out their year of high school in South Dakota. Don was enthralled with the opportunities for hunting and fishing in Washington's outdoors and was eager to help Ken and me discover its hidden treasures.

"You guys wanna go fishing?"

"What for?" I asked. The thought of sitting out on a lake or along a stream for a couple of hours didn't appeal to me. And I still hadn't got over my fear of water, so I wasn't sure I wanted to go floating free on a lake in a rowboat.

"For fish, what do you think what for?" Don handed Ken and me fishing poles. "Here, they're yours, take care of them."

"But it's raining and wet," Ken said.

"Yup, and the lake is even wetter. Let's go. It'll clear up."

Two hours later the three of us were in the mountains on Silver Lake in a rented rowboat, fastening hooks and weights to fishing lines under a light rain going pock, pock, pock on windbreakers, which offered little protection. In minutes we were soaked through, our hair and backs sopping wet. I felt hemmed in, vulnerable, and adrift in the middle of nowhere. A vague suggestion of shoreline, possibly mountains, appeared now and then through the mist, but no landmark could give us a firm sense of where we were. I looked over the bow, where my line disappeared amid divots created by raindrops. I wondered if I fell over, whether someone's hands would reach down and pull me up as they had once before.

The rain stopped about half an hour later. The clouds lifted and loitered high above. Now we could clearly see a steep slope of hemlock and fir rising from the lake on one side. The evening light shown beneath the clouds and splashed against the slope, accenting the thickly forested mountainside in exquisite detail like tufts of a green shawl. The lake rippled like a wheat field on the prairies while the boat's oars dipped in and out, creaking in their locks like an abandoned windmill.

"Let out a little more line," Don said as he pulled lightly on the oars. The end of Ken's pole suddenly took a dive below the surface. He stared wide-eyed as something tugged straight down on his pole.

"You got one!" Don said. "Reel in a bit."

"How?" Ken's voice trembled.

"He's going under the boat! Come on, reel him in!"

The boat rocked as we tried to locate Ken's fish. Chaos ensued for a minute as the fish darted back and forth, doing circles around my line as if it had a plan. Don yelled for me to bring my line in fast before it got tangled with Ken's.

"Criminy, reel in, you're gonna lose your fish!"

When Ken and I had brought up our lines as far as we could, we held a tangled mass of nylon filament suspended in the air between us. In the middle of the mess was Ken's fish, a ten-inch trout.

The next few minutes we sat adrift on Silver Lake with Don hunched over in his red plaid shirt, picking at our tangled lines and trying to extricate the hook from the trout's mouth. The hook had come through its eye from the inside and the barb was poking out. I rubbed my eye and grimaced. Finally, Ken's trout lay bleeding from the eye and gills, its mouth gasping in the peculiar fresh air. Ken and I sat without a word as Don continued to detangle our lines. I decide to try to lighten the mood with an old joke.

"We found a good spot here, Ken. We should put an 'X' in the bottom of the boat."

Ken played along. "What for?"

"So we can find this exact spot again."

"That's dumb," Ken recited. "What if we don't rent the same boat again?"

I glanced over my shoulder. Don wasn't laughing. He gave up on our lines and cut the entire wad off so we could start over with fresh tackle. Then something diverted him from his surly state.

"Hey, look up there, an osprey." Don pointed to the top of a tall fir tree. "I saw it there last time."

"Yeah, I see it. Is it a kind of hawk?" I asked.

"A little but not exactly. Just watch."

After a moment, the osprey took off, soaring over the lake. It hovered for a brief moment, then folded its wings back, and plummeted fifty feet down into the water and disappeared. For an instant I felt my heart go down with it. Would it come up again? In a split second, the osprey emerged from the water as if pulled up by a strong arm and took flight again with something in its talons.

"Look, it's got a fish!" Ken and I yelled.

"Got a nice one too," Don said. "Slicker than a school boy's sleeve."

The osprey made it look so easy—no pole, no tangled lines, just hooks.

Don told us a story about an osprey that dove like that after a fish once, but the fish was too big for it. "What happened is the fish took the osprey right down and drowned it because the osprey wouldn't let go. Musta been mighty hungry."

I didn't want to hear about anything drowning. I turned to my line in the water, looked over the edge of the boat, and saw my face in the lake staring back.

"I'm down there," I thought as I hung to the gunnels and watched my reflection. "But I'm here too, and I'm breathing fine." I laughed and my heart lifted a little.

The next time Don asked me to go fishing, I said yes, as much for the osprey as for the fish. I didn't realize it, but each time I saw the osprey, I felt myself surrender a little more to this new place called home. Each time I threw my line into the water and waited, I felt a new reverence for the lake and an acceptance of whatever would surface from its unknown regions. Waiting and watching gave way eventually to a love for the lake, high treetops twitching in the wind, rivers falling from cathedral heights, new friends and winged mentors like the osprey. And even the rain. I realized I could not really know this land by any other name than a name with "wash" in it.

"There!" I said, pointing.

Don and I looked up. It was the osprey. It hovered briefly over the lake, then dropped in wing-folded freefall, plunged into the lake, and rose again into the crisp autumn air with a fish dangling in one claw. It flew to the top of the same tall fir tree, where it sat at its nest, looking out proudly over the lake and tearing off pieces of fish for its young.

Chapter 4

The Wandering Eye

It was a simple surgery to remove his dead eye. The tricky part was getting a prosthesis with the right fit to replace it. When he got his new eye, I was surprised. I'd been expecting a spherical eyeball like the ones in Dr. Frankenstein's laboratory suspended in glass jars of formaldehyde. This was a concave fiberglass disk with rounded edges for an easy fit into his empty eye socket. It was off white with a black pupil and blue iris that didn't quite match his other eye. Most remarkably, it had a steady, piercing look that seemed forever to be seeing what no one else could.

Keith seemed oblivious to all the attention he was getting, focused with his one good eye on his toy box. I admired his calm, unaffected manner, just two years old. The day he was born, we were all hoping for a girl to balance out the family with four girls and four boys. He would have been Neva, pairing him with the other N in our family, Nancy. This couplet would go with our two S's, Sharon and Shirley, our two D's, Don and Dale, and two K's, Karl and Ken—squared, balanced, and Dutch. We imagined the fun we could have with gender quatrains—a mini-choir in four parts, balanced teams of four for every game.

Neva, nonetheless, came out Keith and messed up our symmetry. He was added to Karl and Ken, and we became "The Three K's," which was easy for everyone to remember but unfortunate because no one had considered how it sounded having the KKK in your house.

Keith wasn't quite a year old when we discovered his right eye wasn't working. He was crawling around hitting his head on table legs and doors, getting knocked over. He'd bawl, we'd roll him back upright on all fours, rub his head, and he'd carry on again before going wham! into another chair. Rub, wham! again. He seemed more clueless than he should be. Finally,

Mom noticed a tiny white speck in one pupil of Keith's eye. She held him in the air, dangling him wide-eyed in front of Dad.

"Pete, do you see something in his right eye?"

They brought him in to the doctor, who confirmed the eye was no good and had to be taken out and replaced with a prosthesis.

But the problems were only beginning. We couldn't get the right fit for Keith. Sometimes his eyelid would not close properly over his false eye, so after he fell asleep, the eye would gaze up eerily from his crib as though watching everything while he slept. We'd lean over him while the eye stared holes through us. "Hi there," it said, "I know things about you that you don't even know yourself."

Also, because of the poor fit, his new eye sometimes rotated off kilter, looking sideways farther than was humanly impossible. It would look creepy if we weren't so used to it. With Keith quite content playing, the crooked eye could go unnoticed for hours until Mom saw it and grumbled to herself, "His eye's crooked again." Then she would pick him up and prod at it with her finger to try and set it straight. With his eye finally realigned, she smiled at him trying to reassure him he was okay, but it was actually Mom who needed reassurance from Keith. His false eye looked back at her, piercing some hidden cavern of grief in Mom. The tears welled in her eyes, and she nodded. "There now, yes, it's true."

If getting his eye to stay straight was problematic, just getting it to stay *in* proved monumentally difficult. The eye socket got itchy, and with the slightest rubbing, Keith could pop his eye right out of the socket, and the eye would disappear into the toy box, under the couch, or down a vent—the ultimate wandering eye.

Someone would yell from the other end of the house, "Mom, Keith's eye came out again!"

At a couple hundred dollars an eye, we couldn't afford to lose it. So, when they noticed the eye was not in his head, Mom and Dad had to put us on "wandering eye alert."

"Keep an eye out for it," Dad said.

"Now, Pete, don't joke about it," Mom scolded.

Following Dad's lead, we acted by pulling imaginary eyes out of our heads and using them as flashlights to find Keith's glass eye.

Sometimes Keith would not notice his eye had come out, and of course, how would he know the difference? As Dad was about to say grace over supper, someone might notice the gaping parabola honing in on the pot of soup and biscuits.

"Keith, where's your eye?"

He would check with his hand, unconcerned to find only an empty hole there. His eye socket gaped out blood red over the dinner table, the concave impression aimed like a satellite dish gathering messages from the vast unknown, as if he could see things no one else could.

For Mom, coming to the supper table without his eye in was one thing she would not stand for. There would be etiquette and decency for one hour of the day, a futile aspiration in our family. So Mom refused to start supper until we found the thing. As we ran off around the house, Mom ladled through the soup, wondering if maybe it had fallen in there somehow. Then she'd sigh with relief when someone shouted they'd found it between the pages of a book or in a rubble of model airplane parts. Finally, supper could be had.

Keith treated the missing eye incidents like Easter egg hunts, toddling around the house smiling as if it were the best fun since hide 'n seek. He seemed to know what none of us did: that these quests were an invitation to partake, as he did, in life's deformities with grace and innocence.

After the eye was found, it had to be washed off under the tap to remove the carpet lint, and then the moistened disk could be wedged back into place. At times we found Keith trying to wash his glass eye in his mouth, sucking on it like a lifesaver. Mom feared he'd swallow it, a misadventure which would mean she'd have to follow his bowel movements for the next few days until she'd retrieve it. So she rescued it right away and returned it to its proper home. Mom wasn't great with gadgets and sometimes got his eye popped back in lopsided so that it stared at the ceiling. We'd laugh and look up with him at the ceiling. "Hey, Keith, whatcha looking for?" He would laugh and gawk monstrously until Mom finally got the thing turned the right way.

On road trips, Keith's eye could cause complications. Dad had to pull over once when Nancy yelled from the back seat, "Dad, Keith doesn't have his eye!" Who knew? It may have never made the trip, in which case we either had to go back to the house for it or keep a patch over the open cavity the rest of the vacation, not just to prevent people from freaking out but to prevent infection.

"I think I see it." Dad's voice came muffled from under the car seat.

Dad, recalling a crisis involving a punctured gas tank on a previous road trip, had an idea.

"Nancy, give me your gum."

Taking Nancy's wad of gum, he wedged it on the end of a pencil and went fishing for the eye. In a few seconds he emerged with Keith's eye stuck to the end of the pencil and held it high. We were as triumphant as pilgrims finding our guiding star.

Some people felt Keith deserved special treatment over others because of his "deficiency," but no thought of the kind crossed our minds or his. He was just our little brother. And like any little brother, he could be really annoying at times.

Though he was five years younger, he often insisted on tagging along with me and my friends, not taking for an answer that we wanted to play alone and that he should play somewhere else.

Keith was skinny and very fast. No matter how much we tried to ditch him, he'd find us and wedge himself into a narrow hiding place right beside us as if he were a part of the gang running from an imaginary pursuer. It was infuriating.

I said, "Don't you have some bottle caps to sort or something?"

"No, I got them all sorted," he said, "and I got the rare ones in a secret box."

"How secret?" my friend asked.

"So secret you'd never find them."

"Under your bed?"

Keith turned red with fury at the fact my friend somehow knew where they were and ran all the harder to keep up with us. Finally, we slowly meandered over to his blind side and took off as fast as we could. With no peripheral vision, Keith's reaction was delayed just long enough for us to get a good head start. We were gone, and he wandered home, finally accepting defeat in his game of "ha ha, you can't ditch me." Some people asked how we could be "so mean to poor Keith," but they did the same to their own little brothers.

When Keith was around five years old, he developed a fascination for the way lawnmowers worked, spitting out grass to the side in long streams. He was so captivated he'd walk along with the mower as Dale was cutting the lawn and let the grass clippings splash over him like confetti.

One day, engulfed in a spray of clippings, Keith was following Dale as he made his way around our expansive yard with the lawnmower. The grass was deep, so Dale didn't see a rock in the path of the mower about the size of a giant jawbreaker. The lawnmower picked it up with ease and flung it right into Keith's head between his left temple and his one good eye, hitting with such a force that it knocked him to the ground. He and Dale screamed at the same moment, and we ran out to find Keith lying on the freshly cut lawn, blood spurting from his head in little geyser-like bursts with each pulse. The rock had hit an artery.

Mrs. Humphries, the nurse in the neighborhood, came running from across the street and said to get some ice. We emptied our ice trays into a plastic bag, and put this against Keith's head as he lay on the ground whimpering. That finally got the bleeding stopped, and after a quick trip to Doctor Simons's office, Keith had a couple of stitches to go along with a deeper appreciation of his one good instrument of vision. The rock had missed blinding him all together by a couple of inches.

In spite of this near miss, or perhaps because of it, Keith was determined to prove he was not handicapped, so he would dive headfirst with the rest of us into the craziest, riskiest schemes.

For instance, there was a gravel pile behind Old Man Tanner's house—the perfect vantage point on a dark evening for a game we called "Nicky-nicky-nine-door." This time Keith was insistent that he be included in the game, so he was. The rules were simple. First you chose a house to knock at. After knocking, you'd run for cover and then watch the people stick their heads out of the house, bewildered, before they retreated back inside. Knocking nine different times in succession, each kid took a turn until the people in the house gave up or caught you.

We watched Tanner's silhouette against the lights of his house as he searched frantically for whomever it was that knocked on his back door. It wasn't really a fair challenge. Although he could run, he had trouble getting up to answer the door, so even Keith had a good shot at getting away.

It was Keith's turn to knock. To our astonishment, he stayed standing at the door for a moment just to add some drama to the challenge. By the time the door opened, Keith had luckily made it back to the gravel pile. People had said Tanner was "as deaf as a fence post," so we could laugh without restraint, watching him go back and forth across his backyard as he muttered, "I know you're out there." It seemed he was enjoying the game as much as we did, but he'd had enough of it by the fourth time and wisely ignored us.

Keith gave us his crooked half-smile. "I stayed the longest." His false eye stared up at me widely. "Let's try another house."

Ken and I figured we had reached the limits of the risk we were prepared to take for one night with Keith along. There would be many more nights with many more houses.

By the time Keith started kindergarten, the idiosyncrasies of fitting his prosthesis into its socket had mostly been worked out, and the eye popping episodes had become less frequent. There was one incident, however, about two months into his first year of school. The event was more traumatic than it needed to be on account of a small oversight by Mom, who had failed to warn Keith's teacher about his glass eye and that it had a habit, on occasion, of popping out and "wandering."

It was during morning class that Keith was reading his *Dick and Jane* book. He rubbed a shirtsleeve across his runny nose, and the eye popped out of his head. According to the teacher, it must have got a good rolling start because the kids heard it coming like a marble across the wood floor and glanced down just in time to see it passing and looking up at them agog as if to say, "See eye run! Run, eye, run!"

The whole class rose in unison as Keith scrambled on all fours after his eye. The teacher, who could never quite get used to these eruptions—such as a lizard escaping from its cage or a paper airplane straying—was probably at her tether's end of a career gone on much too long.

She said, "Keith, come up here and give me whatever that was you threw."

Without a word, Keith marched forward matter-of-factly with his wandering eye to offer an apology, holding out his eye like an oblation.

"My eye fell out," he explained.

The eye stared up at the teacher with its black, blue, and white concentric circles. The teacher looked straight into Keith's cavity and gasped, holding up her hands to his socket as if wanting to fill the vacancy.

The cavity's red lining simply looked back saying, "It's not all that bad, it's in all of us, isn't it cool? Take a look behind the scenes."

The teacher, unable to catch her breath, was turning white. Before Keith could ask if he could go to the washroom to wash it off, she herself was making a quick dash to the washroom.

Once the teacher's hysteria wore off, my parents had a talk with her. The teacher had noticed something was different about Keith's eye but had assumed it was simply a lazy eye and didn't want to draw attention to it and embarrass him. Little did she know how active, not lazy, his eye actually was.

Reflecting later, Mom smiled while she was washing dishes and looked over her shoulder to Keith, who was coloring at the table. She told him what a smart guy he was for how he handled the situation. Keith didn't look up but just nodded and kept coloring, outside the lines as usual, like he had it all figured out already.

Keith took some hard knocks at school. Because of his lack of depth perception, a ball flying toward him could easily plant itself in his forehead before he knew what was coming. But he kept picking himself up and going down again like he always had. After many failed attempts, he accepted that it was okay if he didn't play and simply stood on the sidelines, unobtrusive and alone, a spectator, his head tilted in contemplation with his glass eye pointed to the clouds as if it was being held there by the sheer weight of heaven.

He would be picked last for teams, but he didn't judge anyone, and he was the first to cheer when others made a good play. If humans were given one eye for judging people and the other for seeing the good, Keith was missing the eye for passing judgement.

At times I wished I could have given him my eye, just so he could walk out there and play left field and show them he could do it just as well as they could. And I wondered what it would be like, if I actually gave him my eye and saw the world the way he did. Maybe I would be as gracious and courageous. Maybe, like Keith, I could see what no one else could. Maybe I could see God.

— Chapter 5 —

Scientist Meets God

Sumas was on the remote edge of the world as far as I was concerned. It would require some exploration. From our house at the center of town, my brother Ken, neighbor Fred, and I followed the gravel alley toward Cherry Street, the main thoroughfare through town. Starting at the south end, Cherry Street ran fourteen blocks north, ending at the US-Canadian border before it continue on into Canada by some other name. The license plates of passing cars seemed to show as many Canadian as Washington drivers.

"Cheese heads," Fred said when we asked why. "They're coming to buy cheese and stuff."

"Have you been to Canada?" I asked.

"Of course," Fred said. "Everybody has. You wanna go?"

"Go there now? Don't we need a car?"

"No. Walk."

The thought confounded me—just walk into another country? "And do what there?" I asked.

"I don't know. We'll find out when we get there," Fred said.

We walked up Cherry Street following Fred until we caught sight of the border. The Canadian and American flags loomed ostentatiously on their respective sides. We continued to a weathered wooden structure that was Canadian Customs. A man in uniform looked down at us from a window.

"Where you boys headed?" he mused.

"Canada," we said.

"Oh yeah? What are you going to do in Canada?" He asked curiously.

"We don't know yet."

"Do you live in Sumas?"

"Yeah, can we go in?"

"Where are your parents?"

I shrugged. "I don't know, at home."

"These are my friends," Fred said. "We just want to have a look."

"You know you can't come into Canada if you don't have a good reason. That would be breaking the law," he said.

We looked at each other and shrugged, then turned and walked away. We were peeved. What could be so precious on the other side of the border that we couldn't see it?

There would be a next time in a few weeks, and we would have a good reason to go into Canada—to go swimming. The nearest pool was across the border. We would ride our bikes there in our swimsuits and a towel around our necks, and the guy at customs would ask us the same questions and let us go in. After the fourth or fifth time, they would know us. One of them would saunter out, pulling on his belt buckle as we peddled up on our bikes. When he saw who we were, he'd simply wave us through without stopping us and call to us to be back before dark. But that was for a later day.

This day, on our first attempt, they turned us away. We stopped at Bromley's Grocery for some candy cigarettes at ten cents a pack. Fred showed us how to use bingo chips to get gumballs out of the gumball dispenser. "You save a penny for every gumball!" On the eighth gumball, the bingo chip got stuck in the slot, and the owner came to help us out when he saw us struggling with it.

"Looks like cardboard or something down in there," he mumbled, poking with his pen.

"That's okay, we don't need any more," Fred said.

We made a quick exit with wads of gum in our cheeks and ran a good block before stopping. I noticed a road that crossed the tracks and went west of town.

"Where does that go?" I asked Fred.

"Up Reese Hill, come on."

We followed the road beyond the tracks. A gravel lane forked off to our right up Reese Hill through thick woods. We walked the lane until we came to the highest point on the road, where we noticed a clearing beyond the trees on our right. We crashed through the brush until we were standing in a twenty-foot swath of cleared land that went east and west as far as we could see in a long, straight line. In the middle of the clearing was a square concrete post that came to a point at its top about chin high. One side read, "The United States," the other, "Canada." We were standing on the border.

We straddled the imaginary line, hopped back and forth around the post, and looking down on customs below. The customs officials scurried about like little bugs, dealing with travelers who had "good reasons" for entering the U.S or Canada. They carried on unaware of us, criminals, crossing in and out without a reason or care in the world. We waved down and yelled, knowing we couldn't be heard. If we were heard, we knew they'd never catch us. The intimidation of that man-made line disappeared as we laughed and ran circles around the boundary marker.

Our map was growing. Sumas was becoming home. Yet, there was so much more unexplored area to cover, and I was excited. Mom didn't have to push us outside. It became our preferred habitat any time of day or night. Our only electronic gadget that might occasionally keep us inside was a television with three channels. Our world wide web was outside, where we happily got caught in the web of Sumas's streets and the intricate webs of nature.

Our fascination with exploration moved from the geographic sweep of the town to scientific inquiry of its particulars. And we had to look no further than the patch of ground around our house. Our driveway was a perfect launch pad for three-stage rockets made with tin cans, water, and firecrackers. Our back patio was the set for ball rolling contraptions. We created elaborate courses of shoots, tubes, and levers, with gravity as our only source of power and the junk pile from behind our garage as our source of materials. We'd get a ball rolling, setting off reactions in multiple directions, usually with unplanned surprises as a ball might leap out of an apparatus like a heart skipping a beat. And we'd come away feeling we'd accomplished something miraculous.

We were infected with wonder. The lot beside us was our Garden of Eden—an entire ecosystem of saplings and waist high wild grass. We harvested plants from it to begin terrariums, which we then filled with grasshoppers to get close-ups of a few blades of grass being devoured in minutes.

One bizarre experiment involved a maze for sow bugs that Ken and I made from a cereal box, which turned out so well I worked it into a science project for a school science fair. The title on my display teased, "Do Sow Bugs Learn?" something I thought would incite curiosity in even the most skeptical of minds.

The display included the actual maze, three numbered jars with one sow bug in each, and a stopwatch. I posted a chart that recorded the speed for each of my three sow bugs and a line graph showing their speed through the maze over successive attempts. It revealed no trend, slower or faster, in sow bug speed over time, so I could not with any honesty answer "yes" to my initial question, "Do Sow Bugs Learn?" Nevertheless, glued to my poster was a flap of green paper labeled, "Answer." When lifted, it read, "Not sure yet," which caused a few cocked heads and wrinkled noses from observers.

My one regret was making my display interactive. I invited kids to enter my sow bugs into the maze to see if they could beat the best times on the chart. The idea sounded ingenious at first, but by the end of the science fair my sow bugs were gone. Hopefully they'd found a home.

By far, our most fascinating study started one spring night after dark. Ken, Fred, and I were walking a gravel road along the east edge of town when we heard a chorus of croaking rising from the ditch. After a closer look, we found not only frogs but garter snakes. We ran home and came back with a couple of gallon jars. After several failed attempts to catch the critters, we learned that we struck a higher chance of success if we crept up on them from behind. The frogs pushed their feet against our fingers trying to pry themselves loose. We stuffed three of them into one of the jars. Fred caught a garter snake, which writhed and twisted around his hand until he scraped it off into the other jar. We'd no sooner had our specimens than we noticed car lights turning the corner and coming toward us.

"Cops!" Fred yelled.

We jumped into the ditch and hunkered down under the cover of tall grass. The police worried about kids wandering around in the dark though our parents didn't care. Several street lights had recently been popped out with rocks, by kids they figured, which was costing the town some healthy change, so they had put a close watch out for vandals.

The patrol car stopped on the road along the ditch, and we felt a searchlight pass over our heads. Somebody had probably seen us milling about and called it in, thinking we were the ones who'd been popping out street lights, which we had, but we hadn't popped out all of them. One broken lamp was right over our heads, but the police would not have any proof we were up to no good. We had the evidence in jars that we were simply engaged in scientific study, and all they would have was wild speculation. But our hearts pounded, knowing on some elementary level that man's justice and a boy's conscience were slippery things. Finally, the search light went out, and they drove on.

"We actually ditched them without even trying!" Ken yelled.

"Ditched 'em!" we yelled and laughed. Once home with our animal specimens, we took an aluminum washtub and fashioned it with stones, grass, and water to simulate the ditch environment and then introduced the snake and three frogs to each other. We watched them for several minutes, but they didn't move. The snake flicked its tongue into the strange air of its new home. We figured the sides of the tub were probably high enough to keep the frogs from jumping out, and we went to bed. They were most likely too shocked, we reasoned, to give us an instant display of their predator-prey relationship.

The next morning, when we went out to check on our amphibious habitat, we found the snake there, but two of the three frogs were missing. They must have jumped overboard. But a closer look at our snake told us where the two frogs had gone and why the snake was not moving. The snake had enlarged to twice its previous size with several bulges that weren't there before. It had indeed adapted quickly and behaved like a normal snake, swallowing the two frogs whole. Our excitement over these initial results ran high, and the news soon spread, attracting other kids from the neighborhood. The popular sentiment among the spectators was that we should release the one frog and the snake so everyone could "watch them run around."

"They don't run around," Ken scoffed. "They hop and slither."

We had intended our washtub colony to remain intact for further observation without interference. But the public pressure from our ad hoc panel of experts to release our subjects was intense. We finally gave in to avoid public scorn and potential sabotage of the project by would-be animal rights activists. We compromised, leaving the one remaining frog in the tub and releasing the snake onto the patio. To the disappointment of the crowd, he did not "run around" or slither. In fact, his added girth had loaded him down so much he couldn't move.

Our visitors coaxed the snake with sticks to get a move on until they finally gave up, dropped their sticks, and dispersed. Unfortunately for them, they missed the best part. As Fred, Ken, and I watched, the snake's jaws slowly began to expand to a long, wide yawn as if made of elastic bands. From the snake's mouth, two crumpled up frog's legs emerged and then an abdomen. He was vomiting up one of our frogs. The hind legs of the frog unfolded and kicked before the frog was even all the way out. Finally the head and front legs emerged. It lay immobile for a moment on the pavement as if traumatized by its near death. It tried to hop, fell over, and finally jumped as it had been doing before its overnight stay in the snake's digestive tract. We let it go on its way. It had earned its freedom.

In five minutes, a second frog was also vomited up, covered with digestive slime, in much worse shape than the first. There was no time to see if this one would survive because the snake was in the process of vomiting up yet a third frog from a much earlier meal. It was very dead on arrival and hardly identifiable as a frog. To our surprise, the second frog, like the first, eventually managed to unfold itself and hop away.

The snake's purpose soon became plain. Throwing up the three frogs in their various stages of digestion made him agile and free again. He flicked his tongue a couple of times and, as if being saved from a life of gluttony, slithered quickly away toward the garden. After giving us such a performance and so much scientific data, the only right thing to do was to let him have his freedom. We would always remember him affectionately as Bomber for the clever way he threw up those frogs in order to escape.

From that amazing experiment I grew to love snakes. It bothered me when people pulled up their noses at their mention or when someone used the term "snake" as a put down. Bomber also made me think snakes got a bad rap when God cursed them for conning Adam and Eve, while it was really Satan who'd done the conning, and it was the First Couple's own fault for falling for it.

I went to Dad's study and stood at his desk as he was typing. He didn't look up until I said, "The snake was just a patsy. Why was it his fault that Adam and Eve sinned?"

Dad looked at me wide-eyed, wondering from where his son had absorbed such notions.

He fumbled, trying to focus. "It was Satan that beguiled Eve through the snake," he recited and searched my face. Obviously, his son had been thinking about the temptation and fall of man in a way he never had.

"So why? It's not fair to the snake."

He rubbed the top of his head as if searching among his few remaining filaments of hair for a good answer. "Remember, God turned it completely around, right?"

"How?"

"Well, when he had Moses put a snake up on a pole. So everyone who looked up to it would be healed. And when they put Jesus put on the cross, he healed us once and for all."

"So Jesus is the snake?"

"No, he took on all the sickness the snake brought into the world. So in the end it was like God saying to Satan, 'Ha, ha, the jokes on *you*!' We win, and also the snakes get their reputation back. So, you're right, we should love them."

I stared, and he went back to typing. It was a perplexing story, but I brightened at the thought of Bomber being vindicated. I had one more question.

"Dad . . . ?"

Typewriter keys clacked rapid fire through the quiet, but he managed a faint "yes."

"Is it bad to kill animals?"

"Yes, it is," he said without looking up. "They're God's creatures, so we shouldn't kill them."

He returned the typewriter carriage with a zing and continued typing with a fury, overtaken by a thought.

"But Bomber has to kill to eat," I said. "And we kill animals to eat too."

"Uhuh," he grunted.

I had heard it said that God created all animals to be plant-eaters, but that after Adam fell for Satan, God turned some of them into carnivores, and now the reason some killed to eat was because of sin. But I couldn't imagine what Eden would have been like with snakes that didn't eat frogs. What did they live on, carrots and peas? I also couldn't imagine a family supper without meat. Why would we say grace and thank God for the chicken or beef if it were a sin to kill these animals? It seemed to me something was wrong with the conclusion that killing animals was wrong. Something always had to die for other creatures to live.

With Dad still typing, I turned and left his study with more questions than answers.

── Chapter 6 ──

Abundance

Dad had a plan that would divert our attention away from explosives and obstacle courses toward something more profitable. Our science experiments took a turn toward agriculture.

"You can call it 'The Garden Project,'" Dad suggested as he marked off an area between the garage and the tall grass lot next door for our new garden that would stretch the full length of our property. He had thoughts of freshly cooked sweet corn, beans, and potatoes already dancing in his head as he threw out ideas of what we could grow.

We picked out packets of carrots, corn, bush beans, and a few tomato seedlings at the grocery store and read up to see how deep to plant them and how far to space them. Dad chose some potatoes, which he cut into pieces as starters for new plants. He was committed to doing everything the natural way.

Next, he called Mr. Hoelstra, a dairy farmer in our church, who was all too eager to help. He offered to bring over some cow manure and, that Saturday, pulled into town on his tractor, leaving a long trail dripping from his manure spreader. If you couldn't follow the dribble of manure, you only had to follow the stench to find out it led to the Petersens. Not knowing how much manure to bring, he had thought it best to come with a full load.

"How much would you like?" he yelled to Dad over the rattle of the tractor.

"Just enough to cover the garden with a light layer, I guess, and we can work it in."

Eager to get in the pastor's good books, Mr. Hoelstra went at his task with gusto, yanking a few times on a handle to the spreader and letting 'er rip. The lever he pulled moved a little further than he'd bargained for, and he inadvertently dispensed a two-foot pile right out of the gate at one end of the garden. He then continued slowly down the garden plot as the spreader spit up manure at an alarming rate before Dad noticed how thick he was laying it on and waved for him to stop. Mr. Hoelstra climbed down from his tractor for a look, pulled at his pants, and realized the inordinate quantity of manure he'd let go.

"Ah shit!" he yelled over the rattle of the spreader, not realizing how loud it sounded to everyone within hearing. Local farmers used the word with regularity because they lived daily with the stuff, while I'd only heard my dad say it once when he caught his finger in the garage door. Mr. Hoelstra, realizing the slip of his tongue on the parsonage property, looked up to see if the pastor had heard him.

Mrs. Crouse rose from her garden across the street and put a hand over her mouth. Dad coughed at the smell and waved for Mr. Hoelstra to just leave it and call it quits.

"That enough already?" Mr. Hoelstra asked, looking ahead at the half of the garden that hadn't been touched yet by his spreader.

"It's a little thick, I think," Dad said.

Mr. Hoelstra tsk-ed himself. "Unfortunately, once it's out, you can't put it back in, Reverend," he apologized. "Like an idle word spoken." He glanced to see if the Reverend had caught his subtle confession, hoping to find absolution in Dad's face.

"Never mind, the boys can spread it out," Dad said.

We spent the rest of the afternoon with a spade and wheelbarrow, moving Hoelstra's munificent gesture from one half of the garden to the half that had none. Even after spreading it around, the manure lay so thick it was hard to find the soil beneath. So Dad borrowed a rototiller from Crouses, who were reluctant to let it go, knowing how the rototiller might look when it came back to them after Dad had worked the manure into the ground. Dad went back and forth over the garden plot until we could detect only greenish yellow bits here and there in the soil and could smell the manure less.

The ground prepared, Dad gave Keith, Ken, and me each a hoe and a pair of gloves. He wanted us to "own the garden," so we were responsible for weed control. We were allowed only one artificial pesticide—slug bait. Slugs were a plague in the incessant dampness, and without this one synthetic product, Dad knew the garden wouldn't stand a chance.

The pledge to organic purity meant a lot of muscle and sweat. After only an hour attacking the weeds, the weeds took on personalities—giggling villains that crept out from behind the sprouting corn and beans to scoff at us. Just as we grabbed one of the devils by the neck and started pulling, other devils looking on would hiss and laugh. A dandelion stem would snap, leaving the tap root, accusing us from underground of being awful gardeners, threatening to tell your dad, taunting how they'd simply be back another hot day to sprout again.

The moment for sampling the results of the Garden Project finally came after weeks of hard child labor. Mom sliced up a tomato, sending into the air a tomato aroma like none I'd ever smelled before—from manure to tomato, a miracle. I bit into a slice. So this was what a tomato is supposed to taste like, I thought. The fresh beans and corn were enough to convince the most dedicated carnivore to go vegan.

Corn on the cob became a regular indulgence. Cobs slathered in butter and held between fists around the table, the only sound was crunching, grunting, and slurping—pigs at the trough. Corn giblets arched freely across the table, hitting fellow munchers in the face, landing in Mom's hair, and sending us into howls of laughter. Dad's mouth cleared a straight path from one end of the corn cob to the other and back again in mere seconds, like his typewriter in a frenzy over his best idea of the day.

"See what you guys did?" Dad said, delighted, leaning back to catch his breath. "Fine job!"

The proper dosage of rain, sun, and manure had been a boon for The Garden Project.

With the added nutrients, the volume of produce, tomatoes in particular, far exceeded our supper table's ability to keep up. Just when we were reveling in the fruits of our labor and thought this was the coup de gras, we were about to discover the next phase of the project as we crossed the boundary from horticulture into commerce.

"How would you like to sell them?" Dad asked after some thought. "Make a little money off your hard work?"

It seemed like the logical next move, with corn and beans filling boxes in the garage and on the kitchen counter faster than we could ever eat it all ourselves. The more Ken and I thought about going into business, the higher our profits soared in our minds. We loaded two cardboard boxes of sweet corn onto our wheelbarrow and headed for Cherry Street to probe the market. The Dutch blood in Dad just couldn't let go of the old wheelbarrow, a wooden homemade contraption that created an unheavenly racket down the tar and gravel street. Mom watched us set out with doubt in her eyes.

"But look how that wheelbarrow reduces your overhead," Dad tried to argue when we suggested getting a new one.

"Overhead?"

"Yes, costs that go against your profits. So you might sell ten dollars of vegetables, but if you have to pay seven dollars for a new wheelbarrow, how much did you make?"

Ken and I looked at each other, not considering a new wheelbarrow would have to come out of our profits.

"But you use it too, Dad," Ken argued, "for other stuff, so why should we have to pay for a new one?"

"Well, I get no profits from using it around the house, so I can't cover the cost. You're the ones making money with it. So."

The "so" meant end of discussion. And draining profits we hadn't even made yet meant we weren't buying a new wheelbarrow.

We pegged two cardboard signs to the trees along Cherry Street, one facing south and one north. We started with our sights low, feeling out the market with our below-value price of thirty-five cents for a dozen ears of corn. The Canadians found our little vegetable stand quaint, and they'd stop just to witness the two little American boys with crew cuts and t-shirts tucked into our belts standing patiently behind a card table of produce. Then they saw our quality and our price and bought bags full. We were sold out within the hour and clattered back home for more, the adrenaline of quick cash flowing through our veins. This was certainly a step up from selling Kool-Aid.

"Got almost three dollars already! Including tips!" we yelled as we reloaded.

"Maybe you guys should raise your prices," Dad suggested. "Why don't you try some tomatoes too?"

We returned to our spot on Cherry Street with a few dozen ears of corn and some tomatoes stacked seductively in square berry boxes. We changed our signs to read, "Corn, 50 cents" and added "Tomatoes, 35 cents." It all sold as fast as the first lot, and we were soon adding beans to our business line.

"Weren't you selling these for thirty-five cents a dozen when I came by this morning?" one man asked, pointing to the corn with a grin.

"That was this morning," I shrugged.

ABUNDANCE

Wasn't it obvious we'd go for as much as we could get for our product? The man chuckled as we bagged him two dozen ears of corn and took his dollar.

"I'll be sending the police, you're under-selling my store," he laughed, jabbing a thumb down the street.

"If you sell these at your store, tell the people where you got them!" we called after him.

One day a lady from Canada stopped. Holding one of our tomatoes in her hand, she was so amazed at the size she asked if we had used any spray or fertilizer.

"Nope, none of that, it's all natural," Ken said with his hands resting on the money tin. "Just cow manure."

"Cow . . ." the lady hesitated with a grimace. "On all of it?"

"Yeah, that's why they're so big and juicy," Ken said, trying to close the deal.

"Sorry, no thank you, boys." The lady placed the tomato back in its box and wiped her hands on her skirt.

We never referred to the manure again, except by calling it "dirt" once when a customer found a small chunk from one of Mr. Hoelstra's cows that had inadvertently fallen into a bag of beans.

"Oops, a little piece of dirt got in there," I said with a crooked smile, quickly pulling out the offending particle and handing our customer the bag.

At the rate we were selling, you'd think we would run out of product, but the garden was producing at such a rate we had to start moonlighting door to door, which almost doubled our sales. One particular day, we came home with our feet dragging and our pockets bulging. We had made $18.25, exceeding our goal of $15 a day.

After the miles we put on it, the wheelbarrow finally lost its wheel and was reduced to simply a barrow.

"See?" I told Dad. "It's useless."

"It's no problem," he said and fastened the wheel back on with a U-clamp so that it was still wobbly but usable with some extra effort. "There you go," Dad said, "still no overhead."

The wheelbarrow was never the same after that, but it managed to limp to the end of the season when everything, except for the beans, stopped growing. We dropped the wheelbarrow finally beside the garage to let Dad find out for himself how much it needed replacing. We had saved ourselves seven bucks but paid with headaches.

At supper we looked outside toward the garden and at the boxes of produce on the patio.

"What about all those beans?" Dad asked.

We were silent, weary of the thought of taking to the streets again.

"We're never going to get rid of them all," I protested, "even if we sell all day and all night. We're closed for the season."

Dad looked toward Mom, who was studying the last bean on her plate, a little overwhelmed by the onslaught of garden bounty herself and seeming to know what was coming next. Dad leaned forward and drew some patterns on the table with his spoon. He sat up straight again, phase three of our project perfectly formulated in his mind.

"It's time to get Mom and Nancy involved, don't you think, guys?"

Mom raised her eyebrows, got up to clear the table, and turned to us with a long sigh.

"Okay, let's do some canning," she said.

Ken, Keith, Shirley, and I hauled in the pails of green and yellow beans and spilled them onto the grey Formica table in chrome trim. Nancy placed two pots on the table to receive the snipped beans, and the snipping commenced in a flurry of hands pulling beans from the pile in the middle of the table, plucking off the stem ends, and breaking the beans in two. Nancy and Mom filled jars and worked the pressure cooker while Dad went to get more Ball jars and Kerr lids. We'd be eating beans until next spring.

Our dog Skip lay with his head on his paws, his eyes roving from garden to table. A breeze gusted through the screen door to the patio and offered some August relief. Juice sprayed with each snap of beans, and hands from four sides swam across the table piled with greens—the elements of summer's spent growth. The sun drifted down beyond the garden, sending the evening light pouring in over our shared sacrament, bathing everything in a yellow hue. Long shadows of chair legs stretched at our feet. We told stories and laughed.

The Garden Project was drawing to an end. It had come full circle with the whole family finally part of what we'd given seed to. A pride and contentment welled up in me deeper than happiness. Dad could hardly have taught this from his pulpit because no sermon or creed could contain that summer's abundance. We could hardly contain it ourselves. We were out of Ball jars, and the table still lay piled with bush beans.

Chapter 7

Johnny Ball

I POKED MY HEAD AROUND the corner from the hallway to see Mom and Dad's plan unfolding. Five couples from the church sat with Dad around the living room on Sunday afternoon. The drawn out "yaaah's" and Dutch lilts signaled belonging, as did the clink of cups and saucers, dessert trays, and kids running in the hall. The arrangement was distinctly Christian Reformed, people fringing the living room like a rectangular Dutch doily with men on one side and women on the other. The elements for the afternoon event were laid out—coffee, windmill cookies, homemade brownies and lemon bars.

The plan was an ambitious one, the first of its kind in our home. We'd been in Sumas well over a year already, and Mom worried that in all that time we had not really gotten to know our new congregation. She had an action plan. We would invite five church families every Sunday for gatherings like this one until we'd gone through the entire church directory. Dad knew he would be on inspection as the pastor, but being the center of attention was never a problem for Dad. It was something he often reveled in.

"But why do we have to invite the *whole church*?" one of us asked at the idea of the welcome events. "It'll take months."

Mom was dogmatic. "I do *not* want to stay I-don't-know-how-many years in the same church without us knowing each other." We were not going stay on the outside, Mom said, looking in, preacher's family or not. We would become insiders and not be seen as paratroopers, like some pastors, dropping into this wonderful community ready to exit as quickly as we'd come to some other congregation.

She went into action with a mastery of detail that would have made the most seasoned pastor's wife envious. Going by the church directory, she invited folks in alphabetical order and let them know well in advance so none of them had an excuse to miss out and none of them could complain about favoritism because "no one could argue with the alphabet."

The events were dubbed, "Get to Know the Petersens," essentially our own belated welcome party. The congregation for the most part took to the idea like cows to the milking parlor, some eager for the feeding trough and others dispassionately going with the flow. Wherever there were pastries and coffee, you could find a herd like us.

This first of many hopeful Sundays started with the Ackermans, the Balls, the Brandsmas, the H. Dykehouses and the J. Dykehouses. I had seldom seen my parents looking so bright. Dad was in rye form, laying down his best stories. As I peered from the hall, Dad was telling about the goodbye party they'd given us at our church in Platte.

"So at the farewell they gave me a large comb for a goodbye present," Dad was saying. "The comb had teeth like a pitch fork." Dad was bald with a closely cropped horseshoe of hair ringing his head just above the ears, so the gag gift needed no explaining. The room broke into laughter.

"They gotcha, Reverend!" someone laughed. "Did you keep the comb?"

"Yes, I did," Dad said with a smirk that signalled more was coming. "I held the comb up to the audience and said, 'I'll never part with it.'"

The room exploded with loud guffaws just as Mom skated in from the kitchen with a tray of lemon bars. She asked what Dad was talking about. Mrs. Ackerman tried repeating the joke through tears.

"Oh, that," Mom said with a wave of her hand. "He's told that one so many times." But she laughed to show her support.

In the backyard, Nancy tried to set up a game of croquet for fifteen kids spanning five to fifteen years old. An elaborate course of wickets made from two croquet sets strung out like a skein of geese from the backyard, elbowing around the corner of the house into the side yard. It was a croquet marvel.

Hands grabbed willy-nilly at a wide arsenal of mallets and colored balls. Some of us had to play in pairs. Then Nancy attempted, to no avail, to arrange turns. It was chaos from the beginning as everyone, in no particular order, lined up someone else's ball and sent it scuttling violently across the lawn.

One of the older kids, Johnny Ball, was doing everything he could to stick out in the crowd, striking balls at random whenever they rolled into his vicinity. He sent Kirsten Dykehouse's ball into the bushes near the house.

"Hey, the orange ball's mine!" she said.

"I'm not an orange Ball," said Johnny Ball, "and I'm not yours."

The "ball" joke was funny the first time, but after several repetitions it lost mileage quickly as he continued his improv routine over the remainder of the game—"No, don't hit Ball! Ouch," and so on. Janice Ackerman asked where her red ball was, and Johnny said, "I'm right here," and puffed up his cheeks to make his face turn red. I gave my ball a hard whack in his direction and hit him in the foot.

"Ouch! Right on the ball of my foot!" he laughed, but no one else was laughing.

Ken and I escaped inside for a drink of water, and Mom asked why we weren't outside with the rest of the kids.

"We're wore out from all the people," Ken said.

"Especially one person," I said, "and he won't shut up. Johnny Ball—he keeps telling stupid jokes and he's wrecking everything. He's just dumb."

Mom thought for a moment. "Well, when that happens, you just laugh a little, and smile, and just try to keep everybody happy, but don't make him think he's not welcome."

"We aren't," I lied.

The Ball home sat alone on the outskirts of town along the railroad tracks. Johnny's dad was not a dairy farmer like most other dads in the church. He was a fixit man, taking on small jobs others had no stomach for—unclogging toilets in flooded bathrooms, coaxing raccoons out of attics, exterminating large populations of rats, and pulling wet leaves out of gutters. Few people visited the Balls other than the church elders on their annual house calls, which usually meant trying to ferret out funds to make the church budget, but the Balls didn't have much to let go of.

Their yard was scattered with old railway tools and spikes. People surmised Mr. Ball had done rail work somewhere in his past, an assumption made more credible by his downward gaze and cautious gait as if he were walking the railway ties. And he had a permanent forward lean as though he were being pulled down the tracks to somewhere else more promising.

"I don't care who's greasy, or who smells like cow manure, or who you don't like," Mom told Ken and me when we refused to go back to the croquet game. "Jesus was born in a barn and don't you forget that! We are here now, I don't know for how long, but we are here, and we are going to love the people God gave us whether you like them or not."

Ken and I tried to imagine twenty-some gatherings like this one. We hadn't caught the spirit of "Get to Know the Petersens" and had already scanned the list of families to identify which kids we were in favor of visiting us and which ones we were not, marking on the calendar with a black dot the Sundays we knew the unfavorable ones would be coming.

"It's only for one afternoon a week, so try to enjoy it," Mom said.

"How much longer?" Ken asked.

"Another hour. Just do your best."

Mom sent us out again with some Kool-Aid and cookies. The group had already dispersed and abandoned their mallets, leaving an array of croquet accoutrement like a dot-to-dot page over the yard. Everyone brightened up when they saw our Kool-Aid and cookies and sprawled out on the lawn for a break. I sighed, grateful the first Get to Know the Petersens day was almost over. Under our maple trees, a breeze shifted leafy shadows on the grass like hands trading baseball cards. If this were my show, I thought, I'd pick the kids myself and invite them for night visits, when we could play "Hope to See the Ghost Tonight." Mom never liked us playing the game because it looked too much like a cult of screaming spooks and hooligans circling the parsonage.

Ackermans told their kids to jump in the car because it was getting late. Then a fight broke out between two of the Dykehouse cousins, rolling on the ground in each other's clutches while everyone screamed. There were a couple of pushes, a step backward, and the jug of Kool-Aid went spilling over the lawn. I just let them fight. I wasn't about to try to be the gracious host, the pastor's kid, trying to fix things and make everyone happy.

My dad's wishes were that one of his kids would follow in his footsteps and become a pastor, but the more I saw how hard it was to keep everybody happy, the more I knew I didn't want to be a pastor. His work was taking down fences with one hand and mending them with the other. These gatherings were like that, bringing people together on the one hand and, on the other, accepting that some people simply didn't like each other and needed to be kept apart. But I wasn't like him and didn't want to be.

Nancy tried to get our minds off the spilt Kool-Aid by bringing out the badminton set. After we'd untangled it, she got us organized into a round robin. Soon four of us with racquets were thumping the birdie in lazy arcs back and forth, which lulled those who were waiting into a semi-hypnotic state, except for Johnny, who appointed himself commentator.

"Whack the thing! You're tapping at it like a baby."

The birdie went out of bounds.

"Like this!" Johnny grabbed a spare racket and hit the birdie so that it flew onto the roof of the house.

Someone put a spare birdie into play until it also flew onto the roof. Soon all the available birdies were either missing in the bushes or hung aloft, and play had to stop while Ken and I climbed the metal trellis on the side of the house to the roof. We threw down a hail of birdies and shimmied back down over the eves, hung by our hands from the gutter, and dropped four feet to the ground.

Watching us, Johnny thought it would be a good idea to climb up to the roof and sit on the edge, where everyone could see him while he continued his commentary of the game. Eventually, the birdies all flew up on the roof again and fell into Johnny's possession. The score was tied with the game stopped.

"Throw one down!" said Jon Brandsma, eager to serve.

"Throw what down?"

"A birdie."

"Tweet, tweet," Johnny said, looking around. "Ain't no birdies up here."

"Yes there are," Kirsten chimed in. "You got them all right there behind your back."

Johnny sat with his legs dangling over the eaves, smiling like an impish five-year-old. Ken and I scurried up the trellis again to retrieve the birdies. We found the birdies where Johnny had them hid, in the gutter, and threw them all down.

"Do you want to see me jump?" Johnny hollered down.

"Go ahead and jump," someone shouted back. "Let's see ya."

Johnny sat with his arms folded, the king surveying his kingdom. It was a short jump down from where he sat to a plush green carpet, not a feat worth crowing about.

"Too scared?" someone taunted.

"Chicken! Bawk, bawk."

"What'll you give me if I jump?" Johnny said.

"Nothing."

"Come on, let's finish the game!" Jon yelled.

I turned to Ken. "Should I push him off?"

Ken shrugged. I stepped quietly down the roof behind Johnny, and while everyone was telling him to jump, I gave his back a push, just enough to get him started. The push sent him over the edge in a half somersault, his arms folded in front of him, and he came to a thudding halt to the ground. Everyone went silent as Johnny got up screaming, cradling his arms, and staggering to the back door.

We could hear his cries echoing from inside the house. I dropped down from the roof and glanced around. Everyone was quiet, wondering whether or not to go on with the game. They seemed far away, and I was alone. A pit came to my stomach with an overwhelming sense of stupidity and shame. At my feet, two molds were cast in the turf where Johnny Ball's forearms had planted themselves like a seal of indictment. I couldn't take back the push or erase its impact.

Someone said he was just faking it. Others indulged in the horror, convinced he'd broken his arms. I begged Johnny to be joking again, to come out of the house laughing with his arms intact and functioning normally. If he did, I would be the first to be his friend and laugh at all his jokes from then on.

But now, added to Johnny's screams, a cacophony of panicked adult voices echoed from inside the house. It grew louder as our guests retreated out the door. I could not look at my parents. Undoubtedly, the word would soon spread to future guests about the little Petersen terror who pushed kids off the roof, and that would be the end of Get to Know the Petersens because they'd have got to know us as much as they cared to from the gossip. Johnny sobbed, gingerly holding both arms, as Mr. and Mrs. Ball, without a word, helped him into their rusted pickup and headed for the hospital.

I was restless that night, battling with my conscience and the foreseeable consequences. The next morning, when Dad returned from visiting Johnny Ball at the hospital, he said Johnny had broken both arms below the elbow. They had to keep him overnight to monitor the pain. Dad wore the pain in his sleepless eyes and despondent voice. This was about Johnny, yes, but I knew what Dad was thinking. It was also about him and me as father and son. And he saw the ripples on a pond as well. His position in the community and our family's witness were parts of the equation. He carried a weariness that had grown over the years from raising eight kids who repeatedly defied the limits of credulity and dumb moves. He paced the kitchen floor and then leaned on the back of a chair.

I had one eye on the cabinet that stored the ping pong equipment. A ping pong paddle was a standard punishment. It came as three swats in Trinitarian Calvinist fashion—Father! Son! And Holy Spirit!—with a big wind up on "holy" and a final affirmation on "spirit" as the paddle made its mark as sure as the Apostles' Creed. The ritual was unspoken. The paddle did all the talking.

If ever there was a time I deserved a waffle pattern on my backside from a paddle, this would have been it. But Dad simply leaned on the back of the chair digging his nails into the vinyl. He was as wounded as Johnny Ball was and as I was. Finally, he looked me in the eye and instructed me firmly in his tired voice, "Go get your money, see how much you have."

I got the cigar box from the drawer in my bedroom, emptied it onto the kitchen table, and counted a little less than seven dollars.

"Okay, take that up to Rietkirk's," Dad said, "and find something for Johnny, and tomorrow, when Johnny's home from the hospital, we'll take a walk over to his house."

"All of it?" I asked, looking down at my life's savings. I couldn't imagine spending all my money in one fell swoop, but to Dad that was precisely the idea. It had to be all or nothing. It had to hurt, and he knew the best means of getting to a young Dutchman's conscience was to hit him in his piggy bank.

"What should I get him?" I asked Mom, sadly.

"Well, let's see. What would you want if you were in his place? Get him that."

I would have wanted a new baseball glove, but the thought of Johnny with his arms in casts and unable to use it didn't seem right. I couldn't put myself in Johnny's place because I could not imagine going that long without playing baseball. Guilt struck fresh.

The next morning Mom said she'd go with me to Rietkirk's to help me find something suitable for Johnny, but Dad said, no, I should go by myself and think things over on the way there. It was a long walk but not as long as the walk to Johnny's house would be.

I didn't know what to get and finally asked Mr. Rietkirk for one hundred jawbreakers.

"Having a party?" he smiled.

I forced a smile as he dumped the jawbreakers into a large paper bag. That only cost me one dollar with six more to spend. I added several kinds of candy bars, some licorice whips, a few handfuls of Bazooka gum, Tootsie rolls, and Tootsie roll pops, along with some gumballs from the gumball machine using my pennies. After fifteen minutes, Johnny's present was ready, stuffed into a large bulging bag.

Dad was already zipping up his jacket when I got home. I showed Mom what I'd got for Johnny. Dad took a quick peek inside the bag and glanced up wide-eyed at Mom, who quickly turned away trying to stifle her laughter.

"You said to let him do it himself," she reminded him.

Dad and I headed for the Balls' house together. Nothing was said as we crossed Cherry Street and then crossed the tracks. I felt anxious, but strangely I also felt a sense of companionship with my dad. I knew this was difficult for him too. Having him there eased the fear of owning up to what I'd done. After walking ten minutes, Johnny Ball's present was getting heavy. We stopped as Dad waited for me to catch my breath.

Dad would never consider that what I was doing was paying penance. He was a devoted son of The Reformation. We were saved by grace alone, he'd always said, not by anything we think we'd done to earn God's favor. But he was also a practical man, his theology made of the raw stuff of earth and human relations. For him, grace had to work its way, tilling the clay of the heart, preparing it for love to take root, and there were few things like a long walk that could soften the heart and plant the seed.

We walked the final five minutes to the Balls. The roof of their house sagged under the weight, it seemed, of a God who had not looked favorably on them. Two posts on cinder blocks propped up the porch over the front door. My heart raced. Dad took two long strides to the door, like someone who'd done this many times, and told me to knock. There was no answer. For a moment I hoped no one was home and we'd turn back. But I knew if we did, Dad would have me coming to this door all over again.

"Hello, Reverend." A solemn voice greeted us from the shadows beyond the screen door. "Come in."

"Hi Jordan," Dad echoed.

The house was dimly lit. I caught a smell of wet socks. From another part of the house, I heard Johnny's mom humming. We stepped deeper into the living room.

"Hey there!" said someone on the far side of the room.

Johnny sat on a couch with his arms crossed in front of him in two slings, the same position his arms had been in when I pushed him from our roof. In the dim light, his clean white slings stood out like angel's wings.

Dad urged me forward.

"Hi, I got you this." I held out the bag and took a couple steps. Then realizing he couldn't grab it, I set it on his lap, grateful to have it off my hands.

His wings hovered over the present, awkwardly trying to unfold themselves and wrap around the bag. I helped him open it while I felt my ears go red. I wanted only to turn around and run back home as fast as I could.

Johnny's mom came with a couple glasses of juice for Dad and me.

"I broke both my arms." Johnny held up his arms to me and laughed as if the whole thing was a joke. He didn't blame me, and he wasn't bitter. I was seeing Johnny's truer self now that he didn't have to try to get attention. I felt his gratitude that I'd come, as if someone had finally acknowledged his existence. We were two ordinary boys, who occasionally did similarly stupid things and had to face up to what we did.

His fingers protruded from his casts and fumbled with the bag.

"I'll take a Butterfinger," he said, looking up at me.

I reached in and pulled one out.

"Butterfingers, get it?" he said, wiggling the ends of his fingers.

I peeled back the wrapper and wedged the candy bar between his fingertips so he could grasp it. He told me to pick something for myself, and I took a Butterfinger as well. Johnny smiled, showing bits of chocolate and orange in his crooked teeth. I laughed. His candy bar splintered like bones with each bite and sent shards onto his white slings.

Chapter 8

Sex Education

In Sumas dogs ran unleashed and unneutered, and there was no nonsense talk about what breed your dog was, or if you had him registered, or who the father of your dog was. It was a canine wild west, and that gave us a head start in sex education. The parents of the community were secretly beholden to the dogs for getting them off the hook from sex talks. Open conversation on the subject approached blasphemy and always fell far short of what the kids already knew anyway. A parent's job was to help kids with homework and instruct them in religious doctrine, but on the subject of sex we were left to the classrooms of our backyards, playhouses, magazines, and secret societies.

When I was eight and Ken six, we were shooting baskets at our neighbor Rodney's place, when he announced that his dog Sadie was "in heat."

"What's that?" I said.

"It's what Sadie's got," Rodney explained, "and it's why other dogs have been jumping on her."

Dogs we'd never met felt her heat from far across town and came just for a chance to jump on Sadie. She was suddenly the most popular dog in town. Rodney was sober and knowing, and his words spoke of an awesome mystery. "This is not just dog play time."

Rodney shouted the dogs off when it became too much for Sadie. They retreated a short distance and were right back at it again, pressed on by a fearless abandon. One of the pack jumped up on Ken's leg, grabbed him with his forepaws, and would not let go. The dog's pink tongue hung out unnaturally.

"Lookit!" Ken said, "He's hugging my leg!"

Rodney laughed. "He's humping you."

Ken tried to escape with his leg dragging the dog until it finally let go, but the dog kept coming at him. I went quiet with a mix of dread and repulsion at the dogs' unrelenting obsession.

One afternoon while Sadie was still in heat, we heard yelping from the far side of Rodney's house. We ran over to see Sadie and a black and white mongrel in an abominable pose. The two dogs were facing in opposite directions, bonded as a single misshapen creature, their rear ends locked together and hind legs suspended off the ground. They were helplessly trapped in a death hold. The deed could not be undone. Rodney cried in a panic, grabbed a two-by-four, and began whaling on the mongrel that had latched onto Sadie, causing both dogs to cry even louder, and as they cried louder, Rodney cried louder and hit the interloper harder.

"Don't do that!" Rodney's dad yelled from the house. "They're tied! Just leave them be for goodness sake, they'll come undone by themselves."

Rodney dropped the two-by-four and ran into the house crying. I felt queasy. We had encroached on something wholly other.

Sadie in heat was my first uncomfortable lesson, unsolicited, in sexual relations—unwarranted aggression and strife followed by the ultimate outcome of two otherwise good and decent individuals locked inseparably in pain. Sex, I learned, was a world of mystery and violence, and I could understand why adults did not want to breach these unspeakable secrets. Maybe they didn't understand it either.

So we were left to our own devices and conclusions. We considered the other dogs to be Sadie's adversaries and their behavior to be acts of violence, perhaps due to forces beyond their control, but violence nevertheless. We decided we would counter violence with violence and formed a Kill Dog Patrol, code named it "KDP," and swore secrecy. We considered BB guns but were afraid of taking out an eye. Rodney suggested stoning, which I didn't think was much kinder than BB guns.

"It's in the Bible!" Rodney said, a grave resolve in his eyes. Stoning was necessary, just, and validated by scripture. So stoning it was.

When the pack next approached Sadie, we hunkered down in an abandoned truck bed, rocks in hand. On signal, we flew into action with a hail of stones fired from our position. I was thankful none hit their mark and simply scared them off. To our dismay, one of the dogs would eventually manage to find conjugal agony with Sadie in the far corner of a vacant lot.

The KDP may have appeared to outsiders as irrational as the impulse that drove the dogs to Sadie, but our moral imperative remained—we were protecting Sadie from being ganged up on. The humping deserved recrimination.

The KDP finally died out when Sadie's heat cooled off, and the male dogs went on to more fertile pastures. About two months later we heard not yelping but squealing sounds coming from under Rodney's house. We peered in through a crawlspace to see Sadie there, her bright eyes looking out as if to say, "See and believe what miracles dark things of recent days hath wrought. It's beyond comprehension even for me." Her gaze was serene. As our eyes adjusted to the dark, we could make out a couple of brown and white fur balls with little feet around Sadie's stomach. Two puppies were pawing and sucking at Sadie's teats with unabated gusto, while a third, eyes shut, was clawing its way to that same blissful source.

Sadie busily licked every inch of new life, and then from under her tail emerged a fourth pup, sheathed in a glittering mucous. This one also made its way falteringly toward Sadie's teats just as a fifth poked its head out from under Sadie's tail, and two others followed until finally seven squealing puppies were pushing like first-time swimmers for their share of the prize. The puppies became a daily attraction the following weeks for the neighborhood kids, and we got to know each pup's markings and habits in detail. The crawlspace beneath Rodney's house became indelibly framed in my subconscious that day as a dark porthole to heaven.

I did not make the association between the dog world and human sexuality until late that summer in the tree house, where Rodney opened the pages of a Playboy magazine to me for my first close-up survey of the female body. I pulled up my nose as Rodney explained everything.

"You put your dink into the girl's thing right there," he said with his finger on the photo, "and then you . . . you just jump around."

"But why?"

"Because the girl needs to be sexed to make babies."

"I don't want to help any girl make babies!" I protested.

"When you grow up and get married, you'll have to. Moms go to the hospital to have their babies, but dogs just need a secret place."

My stomach turned. From Rodney's lesson, my understanding grew from the standard "babies come from the hospital" to "Mom needs to be sexed, first with Dad and then in a more technical way with the Doctor," whereas Sadie only needed to be sexed by a male dog.

My vernacular expanded to keep pace with my learning—the word "fuck" for instance. There were certain words that I'd never heard from anyone among my friends or family, and that was one of them. The first time I heard it was in fourth grade when we were playing "Boys Catch Girls, Girls Catch Boys," a very instructive game in the ways of courtship and romance. First, the boys huddled together as each of us picked a girl to chase. You knew which girl liked you because she would often hit you as an invitation to catch her, but if you didn't want to chase that girl, you chose someone else. We chased all over the playground, through the swing set and literally in circles until we gave up exhausted or until we caught our girl, or she allowed herself to be caught. Then the game reversed to girls chasing the boys. Round and round it went, preparing us for future romance.

In our huddle that day, once we'd picked our girl, Dick Veenstra interjected, "Okay, guys, let's go fuck 'em."

"What's that?" I said.

"Just watch," he said, and turned and ran.

Dick caught Dorothy, pushed his face into her cheek and kissed her. She squealed. Then he ran back to us.

"I did it!" he announced with a triumphant grin.

I nodded and smiled as if I understood. But I thought there had to be more to it than that, and I had to find out. When I got home, I found Mom working some cake dough with the mixer.

"Mom, what does 'fuck' mean?"

She startled, almost catching her finger in the mixer and turned to me.

"What did you say?"

I repeated the question.

"That's what I thought you said." She turned back to the mixer and continued working. "Where did you hear that?" she asked over the whirring of the mixer.

"Dick Veenstra. He did it to Dorothy."

"How do you know that?"

"I watched him do it. Dick said, 'I'm going to go and fuck Dorothy,' and then he did it."

Mom put her hand to her mouth. I thought she was laughing, but I couldn't tell with her face turned the other way. She turned off the mixer to hear me out, and I explained how the whole thing had happened.

"That's just kissing," she said finally and sighed. "Did she want him to kiss her?"

I shrugged. "She hit him first, so I guess so."

"So she hit him, and that means she wanted him to . . . do that?"

"Uhuh."

"You've been learning a lot at recess, but I assure you, Dick is full of beans."

"So what does 'fuck' mean?"

"Okay, you don't have to keep saying it."

"Well, what does it mean?"

"It has something to do with your penis," she finally blurted out and turned to the counter to stir a bowl of frosting. "But it's only for moms and dads," she added.

"Is it for making babies?"

"Yes, it is, that's exactly what it's for." She seemed surprised that I knew.

"Oh." I nodded and left.

My curiosity was quelled, but the word itself stuck in my head. The sound had a punch to it. I turned the word over in my mouth a few times and rhymed it with "truck," "muck," "suck," "buck"—all with the same verbal thrust and catch in the throat. But I never used the word again until years later when I understood its various nuances.

The only other lesson resembling anything close to sex education that I got from my parents came five years later when I was thirteen. Mom called me into the laundry room, where she was throwing clothes into the washer. She held up one of my T-shirts.

"I've been noticing the armpits on your shirts," she said informatively.

"Yeah, what?"

"They've been smelling a bit lately."

It felt like an accusation. "Smelling like what?" I said.

"Well, you know . . . body odor?"

"Yeah. So?"

"Well, you're growing up and becoming a young man," she added, forcing a smile, trying to be affirming.

"So?"

"And I think it's time you started, well, using deodorant . . . like a man. Just spray a little in your armpits, like that." She demonstrated with an imaginary can of deodorant. "Or use that roll-on kind, they have that now too . . ."

I rolled my eyes. "Mom, I know what deodorant is."

Then came the clincher. "And maybe you should have a chat with your dad too about things."

"Chat about things?"

"Things like that."

"Like roll-on deodorant?"

"Just talk to him okay?"

It finally occurred to me days later what she meant when Dad and I were driving home one night after a high school basketball game. We'd won the game, the cheerleaders had been jumping around excitedly, and the testosterone levels on our side of the gym had been running high. Dad's face glowed soberly in the pale luminescence from the dashboard. He must have noticed I'd been watching the cheerleaders, and it occurred to him to ask a timely question.

"Have you been learning about the birds and the bees at school?"

"Birds and bees?"

"Yes. Between boys and girls?"

I paused and told him no, my teacher hadn't said anything. It was a lie. Our teacher had tried, once, and abruptly changed course when he heard giggles from the class. I knew Dad was trying to get at the "dad-son talk," but I tried not to encourage him and looked out the passenger window.

"I've got a book for you when we get home," he said.

And that was all that was said on the matter. The book went by the awe-inspiring title, *God's Temples*. It had been making the rounds among the church kids, and Dad, being the pastor, did not want me to hear it last from him. He handed me the book as if admitting to an illicit affair. The details were cloaked in religious language. Our bodies, the book informed, is where God abides—God's temples—and we were to reverence our bodies as his dwelling place. It included diagrams and sketches, which emphasized that God was in the details. For the parents it was like killing two birds with one stone—sex education and sanctification—without having to broach the subject. And it served, they thought, to head off the misinformation we were probably getting from our peers.

The most fascinating thing about *God's Temples* was that it was written for both boys and girls so that each group could have a good look at the sexual apparatuses of the other. So what we'd already seen in *Playboy* was given in stark black and white sketches in cross section, which made sex seem sterile and scientific. It was all there—the vagina, labia, leading to the uterus and then up the fallopian tubes like a curvy highway all the way to two bowls of popcorn—the ovaries—the winning sperm's reward at the end of the race. I held the book at arm's length and looked, and the diagram became a great horned Brahma bull staring menacingly out from the page.

Each turn of the page was intended to expose new mysteries about the biological processes of each gender. Some things were obvious—like, budding breasts and pubic hair meant you were entering adolescence. The girls' part told them they didn't have to be freaked out by their first period, and the boys' part told us wet dreams were quite normal. And another page explained something we had to know *only* for after we got married—though boys could get aroused in a matter of one to three minutes, girls needed about fifteen minutes to get warmed up, so boys should learn the discipline and pleasure of delayed gratification.

A disquieting reverence gripped me at the suggestion that God had designed me in such detail and knew my secret thoughts and inescapable yearnings.

My peers offered apocryphal additions to the book, like the idea that God would strike you bald if you thought about sex too much. Though it sounded off the wall, it did make me think twice because Dad was very bald and had produced eight of us kids. Following the suggestions in *God's Temples* for "self-control of thoughts and urges," I did lots of running around the block that year. Dad even commented on it.

"You're sure getting a lot of jogging in. Keeping in shape? Good for you."

But he'd read the book too, so I knew that he knew what the running was about.

About the time *God's Temples* was making the rounds, our principal and eighth grade teacher, Mr. Bosman, tried one more time to broach the subject of sex. He felt it his duty, before sending us off to high school, to step up and give us a few footnotes to *God's Temples* and some parting words of wisdom, where perhaps our parents had let the ball drop.

He met with us boys first. His slight frame bounced on his tiptoes as he spoke. He had a weak voice, which made him seem older than he was and unqualified to address us on the subject. We weren't paying attention until he mentioned "girls' development." He warned us that looking up a girl's skirt when she sat down was just as bad as actually doing it with her. That created some red faces and uneasy shifting. We were all guilty. As girls squeezed into their desks, their miniskirts crept up their thighs, and we would instinctively cast sideways glances. Or, we'd peek down a girl's cleavage as she reached for a pencil we dropped by her desk. How could a guy not notice and be curious? To give his homily on lechery an exclamation mark, Mr. Bosman said he also knew what we were hiding when we put our notebooks down on our laps because he'd been watching. That thought creeped us out.

Before dismissing us, Mr. Bosman had a final word about language and gestures. I was anticipating a comment about the f-word, but he simply stood before the class and held up his middle finger to the class and frowned to get our attention.

"We all know what this means," he said, wiggling his boney finger. He turned it around and examined it. His thin voice crackled. "I despise this." He slowly displayed his middle finger to all corners of the classroom. We could no longer stifle our laughter, which came out in coughs, sputters, and snorts around the room. Walter Groethuis, unable to hold it in, let out a loud, red-faced guffaw.

"Okay, Walter, you can be dismissed," Mr. Bosman said quietly. Then, seeing that decorum had completely eroded, he said, "In fact, all of you can be dismissed if you just think it's funny. But I beseech you to remember what I said."

We rushed to the door, ready to burst. Dick Veenstra said, "Don't worry, sir, we'll never forget it."

The guys said later that Bosman probably meant he despised sex more than the finger. We couldn't imagine him ever doing it.

During the afternoon break, we huddled with the girls on the playground to share notes on our respective meetings with Bosman. The girls towered above us, their breasts almost at eye level to us boys. They swayed coyly. Bosman had told them they should not wear short skirts because it was a temptation most boys couldn't handle. The boys went quiet, considering the assertion. As a final word to the girls, Bosman had gone out on a limb, telling them, "Keep your panties up and your dresses down." Brenda tug down playfully on her skirt. The girls warned us not to be looking anymore and walked away giggling. In the ensuing weeks, we noticed all the girls had caught the fashion wave and were wearing miniskirts.

I was twenty-two in the winter of my first teaching contract in a small town in South Dakota, back to my roots. I sat at my desk, the wind battering the windows of our two-room school, as I worked on last minute prep for the day ahead. The students of our elementary school were enjoying some free time outside, running through snow devils swirling in the playground. At one end of the yard a group of kids was gathered as they gazed intently at something in the middle of their circle. It looked all too much like a fight, and I sighed as I anticipated putting on my coat and gloves to go sort it out.

Then I heard a familiar yelp from outside. A closer look through the window revealed, in the middle of the circle of kids, two dogs, rump to rump, both panting heavily, trying to get away from each other. They were locked in the throes of copulating, "tied" as I had learned. The upper grades, most having grown up, as I had, among dogs that roamed untethered and unneutered, knew full well what was going on, but the younger kids were thrown into a panic.

I sighed and leaned my forehead against the frost-bitten window, thinking of the myriad of questions I would have to face from my third grade class. To them, I was master of every question in the universe. I would have to explain the morning's exhibition. My mind rushed back to my childhood memories. I was determined to do a better job than the silent treatment I had received from my predecessors.

My chance would come sooner than expected. Zack from third grade rushed into the classroom.

"Mr. Petersen! Fisky and Coco are frozen together!" he announced and immediately ran out, then back in again. "We have to call the fire department!"

My mind scanned the detritus of Rodney's lessons, *God's Temples,* and Mr. Bosman's parting words of wisdom in eighth grade, all of which at the moment were an incomprehensible jumble. It is said that a crisis will always bring out true character, but all that had survived the test of time from my sex education was embarrassment, and all I had to offer Zack was more misinformation, evasion . . . a lie.

"Zack, I know it's cold out there, but they'll thaw out. If they're still frozen together at first recess, we'll call the fire department."

Thankfully, by first recess Fisky and Coco had "thawed out," and apparently the older kids had clarified a few things for Zack because he didn't approach me for an explanation.

"How are Frisky and Coco?" I asked.

Zack shifted, debating what to say. "Fine," he said. He glance up at me with a look of judgment. I had failed him. He knew I didn't really have any answers for Frisky and Coco. He'd get the answers the way I had—from other kids, dogs, and magazines.

But as grace often wends its way unwittingly among children, the next day in science class Zack gave me a chance to redeem myself. His hand went up and waved insistently.

"Mr. Petersen, how do whales have their babies? Do they come out of their spout or what?" he asked, completely off the day's topic.

It was a sincere question. Perhaps overzealous to atone for my recent failures, I explained forthrightly how whales were not fish and did not lay eggs, that baby whales were born through a hole near the tail, the same way puppies were born, the same way in fact humans were born, which confused the entire class. They turned to each other, scrunching up their noses. Zack glanced back at his bottom. My answer hadn't translated very well.

"In human mothers," I corrected, "the hole is not by the tail, of course, it's . . . it's between her legs."

The class laughed loudly as only third graders can. I left it, having failed clumsily.

I wished I had talked to them about how complex and amazing God's creatures are, and about how odd and sometimes scary animal behavior, and even our own bodies, can seem. I wished I'd told them that sometimes adults have great difficulty explaining things—like magnetic attraction, uncontrollable feelings, and pain that can lead mysteriously to something as beautiful as puppies. I wished that I had been the person to look them in the eye and tell them what marvelous creatures they were, that they really were God's temples.

— Chapter 9 —

Playing Church

Sitting next to me in the pew, Ken whispered, "How many peppermints you got left?"

I pulled out two from my pocket, one white and one pink. He held out his handful of three and gave me a pink-toothed grin. About twenty minutes to go, I figured.

People took peppermints to church not just to take the edge off the medicine they might have to swallow. Peppermints also served as timekeepers, so no one had to crane his neck conspicuously to take a look at the clock on the back wall. Knowing one peppermint typically lasted ten minutes, average sucking time, one could calculate when the sermon would end. And considering a Christian Reformed sermon was usually thirty minutes long, with a five-minute grace period, three to four peppermints would do it. Forty minutes induced cold stares from the congregation, along with some shuffling and reaching into pockets bereft of peppermints. Good preachers knew this and, for the most part, abided by the four peppermint rule.

We found other ways to whittle away time if peppermints became too mundane—like counting the floor boards or watching to see if the fly circling around Mrs. Zylstra would get caught in her poofy hair. Or, we'd swing one leg in tempo with the organ and see who could kick the highest before Mom put a hand down on our knees.

Two services with two sermons, morning and evening, were normal fare. They were like the double portion of manna falling in the wilderness and would have to last people through the week because on weekdays the church was usually closed up and silent. And, of course, the manna was in the sermons. They were everything. Next to the sermon, the other parts of the church service were mere embroidery that set the message in bold relief.

Up front on the platform, the pulpit stood massive, donned a gigantic Bible. The pulpit hid Dad nearly up to the knot in his narrow necktie. His head nodded as if on a string from the Bible to his audience and back to the Bible. His hand, as if pulled by another string, shot up every once in a while to emphasize a point. Occasionally, Dad would lean in to the mike and lower his voice to a nearly inaudible whisper, which I thought was his most ingenious technical maneuver. His whispery voice sounded awesome through the old, timeless speakers, which would crackle sporadically among his breathy utterances as though possessed by divine power. I had heard those speakers for so long I assumed all churches were equipped with this special sound effect.

When the pulpit Bible was open, its covers protruded over the edges of the podium as if its words could not be kept from spilling out to the world. The Reformation may have done away with Roman Catholic images, but the big Bible on the pulpit was an image whose significance could hardly be missed. The Bible and the pulpit were one, reminding us that the Word must be spoken and heard and then lived. And though the Word bearers like my dad came and went with the wind, the Word itself lived on in the hearts and voices of others. Dad was as aware of this as anyone.

So, I had "my dad who was Dad" but also "my dad behind the pulpit." When the door to his study was closed, he was the pastor, carefully preparing, with fear and trembling, what he would proclaim behind the pulpit. In his work, he was intense and distant, not to be disturbed. Aside from the rare moment when I had a theological question, I did not often go to him in his study, which was isolated to one corner of the house. But once I found a Dutch Bible on his shelf. He used it when asked to lead a service in the old language for immigrants. I opened it and tried reading. Though Dad was fluent in Dutch, strangely I'd never heard him speak it. I was curious how it sounded, so I asked him to read some from his Dutch Bible, but he refused.

"Why? So you can laugh at it?" he asked.

"No." I was taken aback. Why would he assume I'd laugh? Immigrants were often laughed at in his day, so maybe he'd heard people laugh at his parents because they couldn't speak English and he still felt the pain. If so, he never spoke of it. Maybe I would have laughed too, hearing the strange words from him.

The solemn pastor at work was not the dad I knew around the house. When he came out of his study, like a quick-change artist he was Dad, winsome, fun-loving, and down to earth, willing to tell stories or engage in a game of checkers. This split—my pastor and my dad in one—was a puzzle I struggled to put together.

One afternoon, Ken and I found our church door open and wandered in. I paused somewhat solemnly before the platform, took the intimidating four steps up, and stepped to the pulpit where the big Bible lay.

It was even bigger than it looked from the pews. I tried lifting it but couldn't. Poking up from the pulpit on a flexible metal tube was the mike, the church's secret weapon that had, over four hundred fifty years, given voice to "grace alone" against "works righteousness" and against the pope, his idols, and the payments for the sins of dead people. I blew into the mike. Ken took a seat in the pews to let me know how I sounded.

"Can't hear ya!" he yelled.

I turned up the volume on the amplifier a few notches.

"The pope is the anti-Christ! How's that?" My voice boomed and screeched.

Ken gave me two thumbs up. My eleven-year-old voice suddenly sounded adult and powerful. I found a stool to stand on and looked into the pulpit Bible. The print was large, in a style that made the Bible seem hundreds of years old. The pages, surprisingly thin, were smudged from the fingers of generations of preachers. It took two hands to turn the pages. An old-book smell emanated up, the smell of an ancient faith that bound my Dad to many preachers before him and after him and to the Ancient of Days himself.

The Bible was open to the Psalms, so I read. "The voice of the Lord thunders!" I said in a thundering voice. I startled at my echo. "The Lord thunders over the mighty waters!"

The speakers crackled. I reached down to a shelf in the pulpit, where I knew Dad always kept a glass of water. I took a sip the way he did and looked out authoritatively over my imaginary congregation.

"Keep going!" Ken hollered. "Thunder! Then what?"

"The voice of the Lord strikes with flashes of lightning!" I continued.

I ran to the light switches and flipped them on and off a few times. Then I turned a few pages, stopped on Isaiah, and read some more.

"When they say to you, 'Consult the mediums and the spiritists who whisper and mutter,' should not a people consult their God?" Then I growled into the mike, "Should they consult the dead on behalf of the living?"

"No!" Ken shouted.

"No to which part?" I asked. "Don't consult God or don't consult the witches?"

"What do you think, dummy?"

Then I did what any eleven-year-old kid would do with a mike in front of him in an echoing sanctuary. I put my hand to my armpit and made farting noises. Then I let out a belch that reverberated through the sanctuary like the call of a dinosaur.

I'd never heard laughing through church speakers before, let alone my own, and was enthralled by how eerie it sounded. Ken opened a hymnal and began singing. I motioned for him to sit down with an outstretched hand as I'd seen our dad do on Sundays. But he ignored me and carried on singing even louder, while I tried to read over him. Our voices, rising together in a crescendo of hymn and prophet, belches and farts, ebbed out through the open door into the street—a proclamation like none the town had ever heard. I could understand why Dad loved his times in the pulpit. With a mike and a big Bible in front of him, he always had the upper hand, and I eventually overpowered my congregation of one. But as I was soon to find out, power can be a dangerous thing in the hands of the wrong person, and the person had to live with the consequences of his words and deeds.

It took Dad about a minute to catch the echo of two familiar voices, his sons', wafting from the church into his study. He was over to the church in a heartbeat and stood at the door of the sanctuary. Ken saw him and immediately stood up while I was still talking and belching into the mike. When I turned to see what Ken was staring at, I saw the dark silhouette of our dad with his hands on his hips, hesitating as if fearful of stepping onto defiled ground.

"What are you kids doing here?"

No matter how impressive my voice had sounded in the mike, it suddenly felt small next to the depth of pain in my dad's voice. I said nothing.

Dad ushered Ken and me out of church to the house. He set me down in the darkest corner of the living room and left to think about what he should do with me. I noticed Ken for some reason had disappeared.

I expected most likely we'd be getting swats with a ping pong paddle. There were a couple of times Dad was so angry he grabbed me by the shoulders and shook me until I felt my bones rattle, but he must have regretted that because he never did it again. I sat there in my thoughts until Dad came back. There was no paddle in his hand. He simply paced back and forth across the room, trying to comprehend what I'd done.

"What on earth possessed you to do such a thing?" he asked, incredulous.

It was a question he kept in his back pocket for our most heinous acts. He normally meant it rhetorically, but this time it sounded fresh and authentic.

"What possesses you?" he repeated.

I could see the pain in his eyes. His own son had desecrated the church sanctuary. I'd made light of his life's calling and the very purpose of the church's existence—to proclaim the Word of God. He waited while I searched the carpet, feeling lost in the spirals of its paisley patterns. I needed to give an answer, one that was as sufficiently serious as the question. I could see it was a doctrinal question and had to have a correct answer, which unfortunately was found nowhere in our Heidelberg Catechism. I was as mystified as Dad was.

There were only two possible choices—God or the devil. I knew I couldn't say I was possessed by God because that would simply add sacrilege to sacrilege, so that left only one answer. "The devil?" I finally offered.

Dad wasn't expecting such a straight response. I rubbed my hands on the armchair and looked up into his face, hoping there might be another answer.

"The devil?" Dad repeated. "The devil made you do that?"

Neither of us knew what to say, and he walked out again. The room was deathly quiet. The whole thing had started so innocently— playing church, leafing through the pages of the pulpit Bible, wanting to be like my dad, trying subconsciously to bridge the gap to Dad the pastor. But it all had somehow gone sideways. My mind sifted through the "what if's." If I'd just turned down the volume on the mike, maybe he wouldn't have heard us. If we'd just closed the door, no one would have known we were even in there.

But at that age, foresight was seldom a part of dabbling on the dark side for me. Like the time I lit a campfire under Old Man Tanner's dilapidated garage—how could I not foresee that the smoke billowing from the crawl space would attract some attention? Or how could I not foresee that the fire marshal might pay a visit and give me a lecture on the dangers of playing with matches? Or, how could I not anticipate, while trying to knock out street lights, that in the glare of the light we were not exactly operating under the cloak of night, or that no one would notice our loud cheers following the sudden darkness when a stone hit its mark?

Sitting alone, examining the carpet, I was suddenly struck with another thought—what if I really *was* possessed. Could that be? I knew from what I was taught that no matter what happened in my life, I was predestined. I was in God's covenant, an integral part of his body, simply by being born into it, and the gates of hell could not prevail against that. The combination of my biological heritage and doctrine were a formidable defense. My eternal security was a certainty that couldn't be undone, even by cavorting with the devil.

But just in case, if I was possessed even a little bit, Dad's grounding me would wrest me of any lingering demons until I could be released like Jonah from the belly of the whale. I was just hoping I didn't have to sit in the whale's belly for three days.

I wondered where Ken had gone to in the aftermath. Was he in a separate room getting the same question? Or was I as the older one taking the punishment for both of us? I stared out our large picture window, perfectly framing Mt. Baker's snow-covered slopes like a white shawl, resplendent in the afternoon sun. I felt my heart leap to it.

Mysteriously, I found out, Ken had gotten off the hook, but he may have later wished he'd been punished as I had because a good punishment may have prevented him from doing what he did a few weeks later at Reverend Cummings' church.

Reverend Cummings was the pastor of the Assumption Church, which many in our church figured was appropriately named because "calling it a church was a big assumption." Our churches co-existed no more than three blocks apart. Our only connection was a geographical one, Johnson Creek, which threaded lazily past our church and theirs, stitching us together like beads on a string. But neither church appreciated the symbolic fraternity the creek offered—the shared river of baptism, the stream of life, the flow of justice. Also, neither church could see our shared protestant heritage, how we taught and lived from the same Bible, to be any reason for bridging the denominational divide.

The two pastors, our dad and Rev. Cummings, did not associate, and neither thought much about a possible friendship. It was just the way things were. They each had their own pulpit and their own flock with their own problems to contend with, so apartheid persisted, born more out of apathy than animosity.

What we knew of the Assumption Church was only what we took in from glances out the car window as we passed by. It had a ragged facade, no more than a shoe box. If it weren't for a modest steeple, one might confuse it for a warehouse. On occasion the front doors swung open as Cummings strolled out and arched his back to take in the somnambulant sounds of the creek. But aside from these curtain calls, we rarely saw him. He was a conundrum, popular among his flock but rarely seen in public.

What made Ken's actions at Cummings' church so perplexing was that of the two of us he was usually the bright one and I the chief culprit, whether breaking into the school gym, cheating on math tests, or walking off the job. Ken would not go along with such lapses of behavior without being pressured into it. But for some reason this time was different.

It was mid Saturday afternoon when kids had started on the down slope of sound judgement and were running out of things to do. Most adults were either taking a nap or had tuned in to a baseball game. Ken happened to be passing by the Assumption Church when he heard a horrifying strain from the church organ. This was odd. It wasn't the time for a church service, and the blaring from the organ sounded anything but Christian. The side door was open, so Ken poked his head inside.

There was definitely a congregation there, but not one of God's. Several neighborhood kids were in the process of dismantling the sanctuary— overturning pews, scattering hymn books and Bibles, and tipping the pulpit onto its side. The reason the organ was blaring was because several books were laid across its keys. One kid was taking shots with a BB gun at a clock on the wall. Ken stared in a trance, just long enough to be hooked by an irresistible compulsion. The seed of temptation took root.

"Ken! Come on!" someone shouted, throwing a Bible down the aisle.

He stepped up to the boy with the BB gun, who was taking shots at the florescent lights hanging from the ceiling. "Here, let me take a shot."

Ken aimed, the barrel wavered, and he shot. Normally, he could not hit the broad side of a barn, but this time the BB struck one of the fluorescent tubes with a poof! Ken stared in disbelief as a shower of glass dust sprinkled down over everyone. It was the shot of his life and, like a stone hitting the pond, it set off another wave of mayhem.

"Great shot, Ken!"

Wild cheers and laughter erupted. A couple more pews were upended. When Ken saw it escalating and what he was being sucked into, he dropped the gun and took off, the organ taunting him as he ran down the street.

I opened the door of our bedroom. The curtains were drawn, the light was out, and Ken was lying on his bed, staring sideways.

"Hey, what are you doing?" I said.

"Nothin'."

A car pulled into the driveway. I peeked through the curtains and saw the police.

"What are they doing here?" I asked.

"I don't know."

Dad, always ready to affirm his alliance with law and good order, cheerfully greeted the officers. He had always backed up the police if they had to come down on us—for playing with matches or stretching a string of rubber bands across the bridge. And he had a quote ready for us from the Apostle Paul to defend his position: "Be in submission to the higher authorities because the powers that be are established by God."

"What did you do?" I asked.

The police stood with their hands on their hips while Dad rubbed his bald head and looked down at the stones in the driveway.

Ken wouldn't tell me what happened until later. Then I wondered if maybe he was possessed too. I couldn't imagine him being a part of such an orgy of his own choosing. Maybe it was my fault for getting him started playing church.

Later, I overheard Dad talking to Mom. "He didn't do the breaking in . . . he got in with the wrong kids . . . there was a lot of damage, but I talked with Cummings about it . . . I think we reached a common understanding." There was no pacing anguish or tears of grief from Dad, not even a heartbroken whisper. Whatever the "common understanding" was, it didn't appear anyone else knew about it. Nothing more came of the incident and there was no more mention of it. Ken had got off again.

Maybe Dad considered the episode a fluke on Ken's sparkling record. It all felt a little too simple, too clean, like some smoky backroom deal had been struck between the police, Cummings, and Dad. But the thought of my dad as a shadowy figure acting in the dark just didn't fit the Dad I knew. Publicly, the vandalism at the Assumption Church was thought to be the work of hoodlums or a cult, and that was the end of it. Here was break-and-entry and vandalism, a bona fide crime that paled in comparison to my playing church, and nothing was going to be done about it? No ping pong paddle, no shaking, not even grounding?

I wondered secretly if Dad's response had been a subtle vote of approval for what Ken had pulled off. From the standpoint of a hit job, it was a slick piece of work because no one in our church had to lift a finger to sack the opposition, and everyone could blame hoodlums.

Mysteriously, one day Reverend Cummings and the Assumptions were gone. They had left town. They were there one day, and the next day they were not. I wondered if Ken had helped expedite their quiet departure.

Months later, Dad was preaching on Jesus' parable about the guys who were hired to work in a landowner's vineyard. As the story goes, the workers all arrive on the job at different hours of the day, the last of them arriving one hour before closing time. The twist in the story is that all of them get the same pay, regardless of when they arrived or how many hours they've worked. Naturally, the ones who have been working since sunrise feel ripped off that the latecomer got the same paycheck as they did.

That was how I'd felt—ripped off of fair treatment. Compared to Ken's treatment for sacking the Assumptions, what I got for just playing church was completely unreasonable.

In the story, the landowner has only one thing to say to the workers' complaint: "It may seem unfair, but that's life in my world. If I seem to be more generous toward one than another, don't moan about it, just be happy for the guy who got a break."

It didn't sound right. It sounded like an excuse for Dad. But then, our dad could only love us as he was able to and no better. He was a "man of God" but also a man of flawed humanity. Though he was an eloquent preacher, when it came to expressing love, he had difficulty putting it into words. It usually came in plural form: "Your mom and I love all our kids." There it was, like a doctrine—love is ubiquitous and cannot be measured or compared, so enjoy all the love you get, as well as what others get.

The speakers crackled intermittently. I looked up at my dad in the pulpit, where I had been too with my congregation of one. I had visited Dad the Pastor's world and stood in his shoes, and I thought it must not be easy to practice what you preach. As Dad reached for his glass of water, he caught my eye and winked, and a grin broke at the corner of his mouth.

— Chapter 10 —

The Body

There was a common assumption in the church that a preacher's kids should be an example to the rest in spite of plenty of evidence that any such expectations were foolhardy. It's possible our bad behavior was a form of rebellion against this notion. In my mind, this assumption helped parishioners feel less guilty about their kids doing the stuff they did.

Dad felt the pressure too. As the pastor, he was assumed to be the most virtuous among the people. So, others refused to take up duties in church services such as leading prayers because they weren't good enough. The preacher would do much better. After all, that's why they paid him—to be the most upright among sinners and therefore the most qualified to pray.

Compared to those outside the church, however, our members felt themselves to be superior. We were God's elect, his chosen ones, and the rest of the world was sadly lost on account of holding false doctrines or having no doctrine at all.

Dad tried to counter such hierarchical notions of holiness, believing he, his kids, his church, and the world were equally in need of God's grace. And as we often found, grace shines most brilliantly in dark, quiet places and in unexpected ways.

Mrs. Miller was the quietest person I knew. She was elderly, alone, and happy. She lived two houses over and had a massive yard, large enough for a small football field. She let us use it without asking while she sat in her armchair at the window, contentedly watching the play and scrabble of kids. I seldom saw her outside except to putter briefly about her garden or to shuffle down the back steps to her garage with something in her hand, leave it, and go back inside the house.

What she had in her hand played on our imaginations. The next door neighbors were the only ones who seemed to know what it was, but they wouldn't say. We finally learned from them what Mrs. Miller put in her garage was intended for all the kids.

So, at the next opportunity we snooped around in her garage until we found it—a bag of treats that were hung on a hook above a pile of kids' books. They were for anyone who would find them, and those who found them could extend her generosity to others if they so chose. And the books were her way of trying to join the two pleasures of sweets and reading. It worked if there were Hardy Boys books we hadn't read. Otherwise, we simply took the treats and raced off. There was nothing stopping us from sharing the news about Mrs. Miller's stash, but we didn't want to reveal our jackpot to anyone.

Each time we checked the hook in her garage, we noticed Mrs. Miller peeking through a narrow crack in the curtains at her kitchen window enjoying the simple pleasure of witnessing her design play out. Opening her bag of treats was a new miracle every time—jellybeans in reds, yellows, purples, and my favorite, black jawbreakers that could melt away a whole summer afternoon. There were always heart-shaped pretzels, which we ate under the neighbor's crab apple tree. As I lay on my back, I held up a pretzel to match it to the thatch work of branches above. I ate it slowly and imagined chewing an opening through the tree to the sky.

There was a theological conundrum, however, about the miracles revealed in Mrs. Miller's garage. Mrs. Miller was not one of the elect. We knew from catechism class that, technically, no matter how good and gracious people like Mrs. Miller appeared to be, they weren't one of God's chosen, because in her case she didn't go to church, and she worked in her flowerbed on Sundays. So, any apparent miracles from her hand had to be taken as suspect.

Election was a theological debate that went on indefinitely. Some college kid might challenge my dad just to see what he'd say. "If you're chosen, you're saved, isn't that right Reverend? And if you're not chosen, there's nothing you can do about it, just bad luck, so why should we bother?"

And Dad might respond with something like, "Well, if you don't know if God's chosen you, why not live like he *has*, just imagine that, and let others outside the church do the same. You might be surprised some day to find people you thought were God's elect actually aren't, and some you thought weren't actually are."

The person might then wring his hands briefly and nod in tepid agreement.

It was a Sunday afternoon, and a handful of the chosen were gathered at our house having coffee and dessert at a "Get to Know the Petersens" event. The Johnny Ball episode was a few months past and seldom talked about anymore. We were nearing the end of these events, well into the "Vans" and "Vanders" on Mom's alphabetical list of invitees. I was glad these Sundays were almost over. It could soon be said we'd made an Herculean effort to create the bonds of good will and fellowship in our new church. My mom, chief ambassador of peace, was chatting ebulliently, trying to help the group relax and enjoy each other.

There were no kids my age that Sunday, so I sat listening to the older folk while we ate lemon squares and pie. The church body was in good spirits, coming together nicely until Mr. Vander Plaats opened up.

He was talking freely in his Dutch brogue. Feeling the warmth and acceptance in the atmosphere, he raised his voice so everyone in the room could hear and spoke as if letting go of something he'd had stored up for some time.

"It is clear von de Bible and de animals, yah? and von de . . . von de birds and de bees, dat God intended for de man to be de head of de woman, and dat means de man wears de pants in de family."

The room went quiet. I thought of his daughter Anika in our class, who never wore pants and only knee-length skirts, which she pulled up slightly when she sat to make herself look more like the girls who wore short skirts. I noticed that Mrs. Vander Plaats kept her dress down over her knees. As her husband spoke, she sat tight-lipped, putting a few uneven creases in the napkin on her lap.

Mr. Vander Plaats chuckled, hoping the group would catch the note of humor in his comment, but everyone was waiting for him to finish his thought. Coffee cups and spoons clinched on saucers, and Mr. Vander Plaats took another sip from his already empty cup.

"De point is, de man is de head of de wife," Mr. Vander Plaats reaffirmed in case any had missed his point. "It's in de Bible."

A few of the men added their affirmation with grunts and subdued "yah's," and the women were all silent, except for one. Alice Van Ep, who had been listening carefully to that point but hadn't said much, cleared her throat and set her cup down.

"Well," she said, "if the man's the head, the woman's the neck, and that means he turns whichever way she wants."

All the men turned their heads in Alice's direction, while all the women broke into titters. A grin broke across Alice's face and slipped away again like a thin crescent moon peeking briefly through the clouds.

"Have ya got another slucky o' coffee, Irene?" Mr. Vander Plaats asked my mom.

His wife interjected, "The coffee pot's right there. Help yourself."

"Ya know, Dominie," Mr. Vander Plaats continued to my dad, still feeling emboldened to speak freely. "Vee haven't heard a good election sermon for some time."

There it was again, that word—election. It made me think of stars, the ones you couldn't see because they were too far away, but you were supposed to believe they were there nonetheless because someone said they were out there. I felt suffocated under a blanket of unknowing as heavy as the universe. I figured you had to be pretty smart to be saved, and some day I might be saved if I learned how to talk intelligently about election. Curiously, at that moment, I thought of Mrs. Miller and her occasional miracles in the garage that could open the sky and stop a summer day in its tracks. As far as I was concerned, the way she elected to give us treats was the only election that mattered. We were chosen, and it just kept coming.

One afternoon, I strolled over to Mrs. Miller's to pay a visit to the hook. As I approached, I noticed a dark oddly shaped mass on the ground next to the garage. At first I couldn't make it out, lying in the shade as it was, but as I got closer, I froze, then sprinted back to our house, where Ken was sitting with our neighbor Fred.

"What's wrong?" they yelled when they saw me coming. The look of horror on my face told them something terrible had happened.

"What did you do?" Ken said.

"A body," I said, unable to get the words out.

"A body of what?"

"A person, I think. Come on!"

I felt emptied of all sense of time and space as the three of us raced back to Mrs. Miller's garage, our dog Skip on our heels. We slowed to a creeping walk as we drew near. The body had not moved. We stopped within ten feet, gaping. Then we could see the body was that of a native girl, maybe twenty, unkempt and dressed in worn blue jeans and a vest. She lay turned onto one side, legs bent in a running pose.

Native people were looked down on, considered by whites to be poor and lazy though natives were the ones who worked the berry fields. During harvest, they were housed in one-room shacks on the fringes of farmers' property, which provided them not much more than a place to sleep. Without them, a berry grower knew their business would go under. Yet, they gathered little appreciation. People accused them of wasting their money on booze and seldom taking a shower, failings that could not be countenanced among a Dutch community that thrived on frugality and cleanliness though as far as booze went, Dutchmen drank as much as anyone. Whites didn't talk to natives, preferring to watch them walking down the street from behind their picture windows.

"She's dead," I said, staring at the body. Old fears of dying did somersaults in my chest. I'd seen a dead body before, at Platte Lake, and now another. "I wonder how long she's been there."

"I don't know," Fred said, "but I can smell something." He crept up slowly to the girl's body with a stick and prodded it. The body did not flinch.

Fred dropped his stick, and the three of us turned and ran for home.

"She was probably murdered," Ken said, "and you touched her, Fred. Now your fingerprints are on her."

We had to tell Mom. Once she'd calmed us down and wiped her hands, she walked back with us to Mrs. Miller's garage. The body was still there, her limp hands extended as if reaching for something, her eyes closed on a nut-brown pockmarked face. We all stood back. Skip went up to the body, sniffed, whimpered, and lay down by the girl's head. His black fur blended with the girl's long hair.

"We didn't do anything, Mom, I promise," I said.

"Dead when we found her," Fred said, sounding like a TV detective. "Probably some other Indian done it. Or she just ran from her camp and killed herself."

Mom shushed us. By this time, Mrs. Miller had noticed us, came down her back steps, and shuffled toward the circle of faces.

"Oh," she said sympathetically, and without much more than a sigh, she knelt down by the body and put her hand on the shoulder while she rubbed gently on the girl's back. Then she brushed back the long dark hair and spoke into her ear.

"Dear... Dear... Are you okay?"

There was no response.

"Wake up, Sunshine."

There was a slight movement of the girl's head and a soft moan. Her hands pulled back, and her legs straightened as Mrs. Miller helped her sit up. The girl hung her head in her hands for a moment.

My breath caught in my throat as the body became a living twenty-year-old girl.

"There, that's better," said Mrs. Miller. "You just fell asleep a little."

In spite of her disheveled, drowsy state, the girl looked pretty. She had a kind face. Skip sniffed the ground where she'd been lying. The girl pulled the dog close to her and pet Skip like she knew her.

"Would you like some tea, dear?" Mrs. Miller asked.

The girl winced.

"Come, try to stand up."

Mrs. Miller applied all of her small frail body to hoist her up as Mom helped. The girl stood and took a couple of tentative steps. Mrs. Miller spoke quietly to her, words we could not hear, not wanting to embarrass her before her audience.

"Why don't you come into the house, and I'll make you some tea," Mrs. Miller told the girl.

She held on, wobbling between Mom and Mrs. Miller, who walked her slowly to the house. As Mrs. Miller disappeared into the house with the girl, I saw something drop from the girl's clothing. It was a pretzel. Skip lay down at the door as if in watch of the girl's recovery.

"Is she drunk?" Ken asked, but Mom didn't answer.

My breathing grew deeper and steadier, and my chest expanded, like a river swelling. I felt suddenly that I knew things I didn't known before, things I would have to hold inside because I didn't know how to talk about them. Everything seemed more vivid, more real—the imprint of the girl's body in the grass, the worn boards on the garage, and a broken window I'd never noticed before with sharp edges outlining a hole to the inside of the garage. I peeked inside. There were no treats on the hook.

As we walked home, the breeze did not feel as it usually did. It did not go over and around me but into me, filling me. My head was swimming. I couldn't stop thinking about the girl with nut brown skin, the garage, and Mrs. Miller's miracle.

— Chapter 11 —

Arthur

Arthur Flannigan focused intently on his ball, dribbling awkwardly, using the entire driveway to get a run at the basket. Then he held his ball, ran a few more steps, and at the last second tossed up a wild shot with a bizarre combination of arm and leg movements.

"It's my duck shot!" he shouted. "My dad taught me."

His "duck shot" flew crazily off to the right. He grabbed his ball, took several steps backward down the driveway, and stared down the basketball hoop with his best evil eye. He went at the basket again. This time his duck shot careened left off the backboard.

I was astonished at Arthur's unrelenting determination, expended to so little effect, and didn't know whether to laugh or feel sorry for him. I was twelve and Arthur nine. I could have offered a few tips, but he would not take advice from me any more than I would from a duck. I knew what a good basketball move was, and this was duck poop and should have embarrassed him, but his self-confidence knew no bounds. Arthur, it seemed, could never shift out of the only mode he knew—calling attention to himself in every sport no matter how ridiculous he came off doing it.

And then there was baseball. One balmy Saturday, Arthur sauntered onto the playing field in the middle of a game in his fresh-out-of-the-box Yankees baseball cap. But the cap was secondary. He pulled up his pant legs and announced, "Hi! I'm ready for you! My dad got me new shoes!"

He flashed a big toothy smile that matched his new white sneakers. We put him safely in right field. The first ball hit his way rolled past him while he was bent over rubbing smudges off his new shoes. He looked up, wondering why everyone was yelling at him.

Another day we saw him in the lane, sobbing. He had fallen from his bike. "I broke my hand!" He turned pirouettes and grimaced, holding his wrist as if his hand might fall off. We ran to inspect his injury.

"Don't touch it, stand back," he shouted, giving himself a wide berth for his stage.

The next day he showed up at the ball field with his hand taped and gingerly put on his glove. When it came time to reach over his head for a fly ball, he seemed to have forgotten his hand was broken as the ball hit his glove and tumbled out.

"I almost had that one!" he shouted, ignoring the ball beside him on the ground.

Often he would announce at full volume one of his latest acquisitions. He got a real bow and arrow set that he couldn't take out of the house, he said, because his dad had just brought it back from the Amazon.

"They've got Indians there, you know," Arthur assured us with a severe look.

It was doubtful his dad had brought back a bow and arrow set from the Amazon. Traveling much further than the fridge was not on his itinerary. He was 400 pounds plus. After he lifted himself from the rocking chair, it would be an accomplishment if he could haul his majestic girth, in a slow rocking motion, from the porch to the kitchen for a bologna sandwich and lemonade, softly whistling a favorite aria before teetering back to the porch like a metronome on *largo*. Arthur's mom was only slightly smaller than her husband. I never saw her get up from her chair at all.

For poor Arthur, you could say he was cursed by being the Flannigan's only child, getting more attention than was healthy for any kid. Arthur's situation was beyond my understanding. In a family of eight, any one of us might go a whole day without any special attention from our mom or dad other than "Got your lunch?" or "Don't hit your brother." Mom didn't even get our names straight half the time, stammering through her entire catalogue of kids before putting the right name to the right face. We might accidentally get the Christmas present intended for someone else. Or, she might lose track of which of us she'd already served supper—one of us would get seconds while the other sat open-mouthed waiting for firsts, like a baby bird peeping inaudibly through the cacophony in the nest. We were in disbelief at how often Arthur got exactly what he wanted for no particular occasion, always brand new, while getting second-hand stuff, for us, was as commonplace as getting leftovers for supper.

Mr. Flannigan promised his son he would be a professional football player one day, even better than he himself had been. There was nothing about Arthur's dad, however, other than his massive frame, that spoke of football prowess. To get Arthur to become a star athlete Mr. Flannigan provided him every gadget that could possibly prove beneficial for excelling to the Hall of Fame. Along with the equipment, Mr. Flannigan dished out a heavy diet of discipline that was as capricious as Arthur's wants and demands. He'd send Arthur to his room one minute, grounding him for the rest of the day for complaining his football was no good and he needed a new one. Then he'd call Arthur back outside two minutes later and tell him to inflate the ball and show his best kick.

I was unable to appreciate how hard all of this may have been for Arthur. The only thing I understood was that he was a spoiled little brat who thought he was the centre of the universe and that he needed to be brought down a few pegs. In short, the package Arthur came in did not naturally endear anyone to him.

If we complained about playing with Arthur, Mom would give almost the same response she gave about Johnny Ball. "Just try a little harder. He just needs a friend."

"Try a little harder" was a formula that never worked with Arthur. The harder you tried to be his friend the more he seemed to drown himself in a swamp of self-congratulation or self-pity, depending on the moment. We didn't have a name for his problem, but we assumed the only real cure for it was to stuff wet leaves down his pants and send him home.

Arthur and his dad were, in my mind, the same person, just different in size. Arthur, like his father, waddled with his arms hanging abnormally wide from his side to make room for an extra wide load, which Arthur didn't really have. It was just the way he'd learned how to walk from his dad.

And there was the voice. You could hear Mr. Flannigan's roar in Arthur's voice because Arthur shouted in normal conversation just like his father, who shouted whether standing blocks away or right in front of you. He would bellow from their front porch for Arthur to come home, his voice resonating like a foghorn from his barrel chest as he repeated, "Arrr-thurrrr!" drawn out in a mournful, falling two-tone call. Arthur's name floated across the neighborhood in waves, like fog itself, menacing, rolling over the rooftops into the nooks and crannies of every backyard, tree fort, and doghouse. If the Foghorn kept sounding and Arthur didn't respond, one of us would answer back on Arthur's behalf.

"What do you want?" one of us would shout.

"Come home, you have to eat!"

"No, I'm busy!" we answered, knowing Foghorn Flannigan never took "no" for an answer.

"You come home right now!"

"No, I'm not hungry!"

"You'll come home and you'll eat your lunch, or I'm gonna whop you and I'm gonna whop you good!"

"Go ahead and whop me! I'm not coming!"

Later in the afternoon, Arthur showed up at the baseball field in his new shoes and Yankees cap with no idea why his dad had got so angry at him.

"I got a good whopping," he said, rubbing his butt and grinning proudly as though he'd taken one for the team.

We were playing football one day when we saw a kid in helmet and pads coming a block away. No one needed to be told who it was. Who else would wear a helmet and football pads to a neighborhood football game? Who among us could afford them?

These games normally started when someone would grab a ball and start throwing it around until more kids showed up without needing to be asked. If we went out in the rain, we still managed to attract a crowd. We'd look for the wettest, muddiest spot for a "mud ball" game and come home looking like sasquatches. Arthur was the only one who needed to be invited. He just didn't know it.

The day Arthur showed up in his helmet and pads we were playing a game of light tackle on Mrs. Millers expansive plush yard. Arthur's pads hung from his shoulders like wilted lettuce while his bright red helmet wobbled precariously on his head, a tomato ready to roll off its lettuce leaf. We stopped and stared at the delicacy approaching us.

"You know who I am?" Arthur asked, flashing his big white teeth, thinking we wouldn't recognize him. He gave a roar and rocked on his feet, scanning his audience.

"Let's see . . . a duck?" somebody asked.

"Nope."

"Mr. Magoo?"

"Nope."

"You're quarterback for the Vikings," someone said, "and we're going to kick your butt."

"Hey, I know. You're a girl that went and got a whole load o' football crap that was twice her size."

"Nope," Arthur said, enjoying the attention. "It's me!" He pulled off his helmet with theatrical flair and chuckled. We feigned surprise, and somebody told Arthur he could sit out and join us for the next game, while we knew another game probably wouldn't happen as we'd about had enough. But Arthur wouldn't take the hint and asked who wanted him on their side. We finally took him on our team even though we understood the liability. Our enthusiasm faded as both teams huddled. It was my turn as quarterback.

Fred nudged me and said, "Give Arthur the ball because he's fresh."

Arthur smiled, seeing somebody believed in him, but everyone knew it was a set up.

"Okay," I said, giving in. "Arthur, you ready?"

Arthur almost jumped out of his pads with anticipation as we broke the huddle. The glow behind his mask told the other team exactly who was getting the ball. They were ready for him. The ball was snapped, I handed it to Arthur, and he stalled as if stunned by the spotlight on his first stage. I gave him a push.

"Go!" I said.

Arthur gave a low roar and ran wobbling under the weight of his accoutrement into a wall that was the entire opposing team. He fell on his own with little resistance, and we watched him go down as if he were Captain Kirk—*must not . . . let . . . anyone . . . tackle me*—in slow motion, first to his knees, then onto one elbow, then the other, and finally all the way down with his face guard planted in the soft turf.

Arthur lay motionless for a few seconds, the ball in his clutches. Someone had clearly taught him to protect the ball at all costs. We waited, hands on our hips, for Arthur to get up and give us a commentary on the play. We heard a quiet whimper as he slowly staggered upright, a wad of grass stuck in his face guard, both arms around the ball as if it were a baby.

"You crying?" a girl from the other team asked. "You went down by your own self. You got pads on, and we didn't even tackle you! How could that hurt?"

But she didn't know Arthur like I did. Without a word and without removing the mud from his face guard, Arthur broke from our circle. He did not glance back as he headed for home, his cries growing louder with each step. Just then the Foghorn sounded from the Flannigan house.

"Arrr-thurrrr!"

"Coming!" somebody yelled. "Hold your ten-gallon pants on!"

Sure, if we had been anywhere near mature, we would have recognized how tortured poor Arthur was, but this was a lot to ask of kids, and Arthur was his own worst enemy. My little brother Keith was the only one who tried to be his friend. But out of the blue one day, Arthur came to our house with his fists clenched, wanting to challenge Keith to a fight. Nobody, least of all Keith, understood what had set him off, but whatever it was had rendered him speechless. He was seeing red. Keith, after Arthur's insistence, finally obliged him, and they locked into a wrestling match. Keith was just a scrawny kid, much smaller than Arthur, but within a few seconds Keith was sitting on him and had him pinned to the ground. He started sobbing, Keith let him up, and Arthur began the familiar walk home.

Certain kids in the neighborhood, when they saw a wounded animal, would pounce. Some took out their displeasure with Arthur by hitting Flannigan's house with tomatoes on Halloween night. Such holiday pranks were commonplace in Sumas—soaping windows, breaking pumpkins, throwing toilet paper over trees—but tomatoes were the worst, dripping from Flannigans' windows and porch posts like bad mascara. No one knew who'd done it, but Arthur's dad thought he had a good idea who it was. A few days later, he saw me, along with a couple of neighbor kids, scuffing down the street past his house. He waddled out purposefully onto the porch and called us over.

"Were you kids around here on Halloween?" he started.

"I guess so," I answered, "at some point."

"Not me," the other kids answered promptly.

"It took me three hours to clean those tomatoes off my house," he boomed, projecting a large finger behind him at his now sparkling house.

"Tomatoes?" I said.

The others echoed, "Tomatoes?"

"Don't pretend you don't know what you did." His breathing became so heavy I thought Foghorn might fall off the edge of his porch from hyperventilating.

I tried to picture 450-pound Mr. Flannigan on a ladder washing tomatoes off his house and thought it must have been quite some ladder to hold him up for three hours. He wagged his finger at us and paced back and forth, the floor boards on his porch groaning their united disapproval while he delivered a course of wrath and fury that would make a preacher blush.

"Your father would be ashamed of you," he shot at me with a finger, fury in his eyes.

"But I didn't—"

"Throwing tomatoes at your neighbour? Is this the behaviour of Christian kids? And a preacher's kid too!"

"But—"

"This is the behaviour of hooligans! And you have the *gall* to target your indecency at Arthur, your very own *friend*?"

At that moment, on cue, through the screen door behind Mr. Flannigan and onto the stage waddled the son, taking his place next to the father. Arthur's arms hung at his sides like two parentheses, a foreshadowing of the Foghorn to come. Father Foghorn bellowed, filling the air with timely crescendos and diminuendos. His voice cracked and we thought he might cry.

"I'm trying to raise my son to be a real man, and you're trying to make him a dishonorable, selfish person!"

Arthur stood stone faced. We could say nothing and left them standing there side by side on the porch.

The day Arthur called me out of our house to show me his duck shot, I thought, it might be an opportunity to show him some of the good will Mom had beseeched of us. And his was one of the only homes with a good basketball hoop. I sighed, grabbed my ball, and followed him to his house.

While he was dribbling toward the basket for the twentieth time, he said between puffs and pants, "My dad showed me . . . how to do it." His duck shot caromed off the bottom of the rim right into my hands. It was a brand new Spalding, the "official ball of the NBA."

"Here, give it to me!" he said impatiently, slapping the ball away from me and backing up for another run at the basket. "It's going to be my secret shot in the pros!"

Controlled by a force beyond himself, he pressed on with greater intensity, each shot more erratic than the last. He paused, sweating with exhaustion. I threw up a few shots with my Wilson basketball, the one my parents had bought for Ken and me at the beginning of basketball season.

It had gone bald from daily use, the small nubs worn off and the "Wilson" logo only vaguely visible anymore. But when we felt it in our hands, it was more than a ball. It represented shared experience that had bonded us as brothers and friends.

I watched Arthur, completely absorbed in his duck shot, on his way to the NBA. I was unable to take a shot myself. I thought of beaning him with my ball and pretend it was an accident just to get him to stop. But I had learned from Johnny Ball that doing stupid things to kids I didn't like, like pushing them off the roof, could lead me on a long road of grief.

I managed finally to take a shot, and my ball bounced in Arthur's direction. But rather than throw it back to me, he flipped my ball wildly out of his way. It flew over his garage roof and came down abruptly in a pile of old boards. I went to retrieve it and found our Wilson impaled on a nail sticking out of one of the boards. I held up my ball in disbelief with the board firmly attached.

"Hey, wow! Look at that!" Arthur laughed when he saw the board fastened to my ball like a pit bull.

Even before dislodging my ball, I felt my heart sink, knowing it was done for. I pulled it off the nail, and the air escaped in a long hiss. Arthur carried on without a word of remorse or apology, unable to make the connection between his careless toss and my dead ball. My face flushed red with anger. No patch job would bring back the familiar feel and lustre to our ball.

I thought of things I could do to Arthur to make him pay, but I didn't. I did not go up to Arthur and flatten him like he'd flattened my ball. I did not tell him he was a selfish, spoiled brat. I did not interrupt him from his "duck shot" trance by taking his clean new Spalding and impaling it on the same nail that had taken my Wilson. Nor did I grab his Spalding and walk to the bridge with him screaming at me while I held his ball over Johnson Creek. And I did not drop it in the creek and watch it float away and tell him it was no great loss because his dad would get him another one anyway even though his stupid duck shot was a waste of time and becoming a basketball player was nothing but an insane dream. I knew I could hurt him, but he was so used to being hurt I doubted anything I could do would affect him.

I turned and walked home with my flattened ball, kicking my feet through the leaves on the sidewalk. By the time I reached the house, my anger had turned to sadness for Arthur because I thought he might never be able to share a basketball with anyone like I did with Ken. I could finally feel the suffering he'd been carrying since his dad first looked at him and saw an NBA superstar.

— Chapter 12 —

Blindsided

I ROTATED MY HEAD SLOWLY back and forth, experimenting with my new glasses. My sixth grade classmates appeared warped into parabolic shapes, passing by like fish in a fishbowl. I tried glancing sideways beyond the periphery of the black frames, where everything looked like it did yesterday, a bit hazy. Ahead, was a new world, the world through artificial lenses, which I was now learning could as easily clarify reality as distort it. My new glasses felt awkward and heavy, like an extra appendage. The upside was that I was getting attention. My classmates were stopping and smiling and staring into my lenses.

"Hey, Karl, can you see me?" Eugene said, louder than necessary.

"I can hear you just fine," I said.

Some laughed, their mouths looking abnormally large, their braces sparkling radiantly as though I was seeing them for the first time. I wondered if this was what the flies saw looking up when we fried them with magnifying glasses under the sun. Would my glasses burn out my eyes, I wondered, if I looked up at the sun?

I removed my spectacles, rubbed my nose, and put them on again. The rectangular black frames slipped easily over my larger than average ears as if my ears had been made for this very purpose and had been waiting eleven years for this moment. I was the latest in our family to discover the wonders of clear vision. Everything was defined with an abnormal crispness. The chalk in Mr. Tjoelker's hand was starkly white, and his writing was perfectly legible. But I was to discover that no matter how remarkably they improved my vision, my glasses could not spare me from getting blindsided.

For one thing, I thought the attention I was getting from my glasses might give me some special status among my classmates, but I couldn't have been more wrong. I was already the "city slicker" in a crowd of farm kids, and few of them wore glasses themselves. So now I was not only the smallest, skinniest kid in class, but after adding the glasses, it was a small jump from being city slicker to class dork.

Except for one person—Sharlene. She thought I looked great. Sharlene was the cutest, nicest girl in the class, maybe in the whole school, with or without my glasses on.

The moment I first noticed her interest, I was sitting minding my own business when I felt a tap on my shoulder. I crouched instinctively, waiting for someone to flick my ears or knock my glasses off if I dared turn around. I looked back slowly over my shoulder, and there was Sharlene. She was smiling, not teasingly but with a generous, genuine smile.

"I like your glasses," she said brightly.

I waited for the punchline, but it didn't come. She meant it.

A few days later Mr. Tjoelker decided to change our seating, and Sharlene ended up in the seat right behind me. Now what were the chances of that? I found out it was not due to chance at all but was a matter of intentional planning. The teacher had put Sharlene and Marilyn in charge of the new arrangement. So, she had *chosen* to sit behind the little dorky kid with glasses. Sharlene, the girl every boy looked at when they thought about girls, had chosen me.

She started passing me notes asking me about answers to math problems. At first I thought this might be a game to get answers, but the answers were simple ones that she had to already know. Her purpose had to be that she actually wanted me for real. Then the notes became more personal, like comments about how smart I looked, and then the notes became whispers about what the other girls were saying about what we "were." I turned slowly in my seat.

"What *are* we?" I whispered, really wanting to know.

"I don't know," she said and smiled.

I blushed. I kept my distance the rest of the day while my feelings were doing Olympic gymnastics in my stomach, eventually rising to the podium in my chest to accept the gold, where my feelings remained blissfully for the rest of the week.

For a couple of weeks following, I existed in a blue haze of sixth grade inebriation without a clue about how a girlfriend and boyfriend were supposed to behave, if that's what we were. I'd been moving about quite content in my boys' world—making model airplanes, shooting my BB gun, and having farting contests with my brothers. And then my equilibrium had met unforeseen disturbance, but it was an intrusion that I surprisingly didn't have any objection to. I was suddenly in another world of odd and terrifying feelings, on another planet where I had to learn how to breathe.

I was so incapacitated that I forgot my glasses a couple of times, and each time Sharlene noticed—she noticed—and she told me I should run back home and get my glasses, which I did, to please her. This was a new wrinkle. I'd never listened to what any girl, not even my older sisters, told me to do, which was more evidence that something weird and otherworldly was going on.

It got worse rather than easier. It would be accurate to say Sharlene was becoming the lens through which I was seeing everything—every math problem, baseball game, song, or Hershey's kiss. Every sensation was energized by Sharlene. Even at eleven, I knew I was treading on treacherous ground, but the unfortunate truth was she had blindsided me, and there was nothing I could do about it. She was the train to distant lands that had come into the station twenty minutes early. I hadn't even had a chance to check my bags. I simply had to hop on board or miss the ride.

Once I'd calmed down a little, I realized my new situation also required action, making things happen in some way. I had to make some kind of move—like walk with her at recess, or pick blackberries with her, or bring the blackberries to her *after* I picked them. Giving her a ring would probably scare her off. It would simply be waving a flag to everyone—"Hey, look over here! Sharlene's got a ring. Let's find out who put it on her finger and pick on him." And where would I get a ring anyway? And what would it mean? Rings were for people getting married—she'd never forgive me for such a stupid move.

"What's your answer for number three?" she whispered, resting her hand on my shoulder.

I shivered at her touch. Then I knew what it was that was missing—a touch from me, or several touches. Perhaps even, I needed to kiss her. That would for sure define what we were. It was exactly what I would do as soon as I saw the chance.

My next words wavered in and out of falsetto, not simply because my voice was changing but because Sharlene had moved her hand from my shoulder onto my hand.

"Uh . . . number three answer?" I wavered. "It's . . . I think, four hundred thirteen, or around there . . . but I don't know . . . a more touch, I mean, a touch more than that, maybe." My words felt like a budgie flapping in its cage. "Are you sure you don't know this one?"

She giggled nervously. "You're funny."

Her hand was warm. I wanted her to pull it away and at the same time to hold it there. A siren was going off in me as I felt the stares of twenty-six other pairs of eyes. I felt the ink well on her desk beneath my hand and wanted to crawl down into it and hide. But then I realized that would put me *inside* her desk, which would be much too close. I wanted to run. I glanced down and noticed how our desks were fastened to skids as an inseparable pair. I wanted the skids to break apart and become skis to whisk us away in opposite directions, with some reindeer added to take me to the North Pole.

By the time school let out I'd regained my composure. I determined that I had to move forward. If I was going to kiss her, I would have to scout out a private place to do it. I walked up Johnson creek to the woods near the edge of town, where there was a wood footbridge spanning the creek. Along the bank was a willow tree with its branches draping over the creek, making a naturally secluded spot. I found a good sitting log in the bushes and dragged it under the willow. A kid no more than five saw me and cocked his head.

"What are you doing with that big log?"

"Nothing," I said, "making a seat."

"Can I sit on it?"

"Sure, go ahead," I said. "But if you ever see me sitting on it with someone else, I don't want you to come around, okay. You just go the other way."

"Okay. What for?"

"Never mind what for."

I found some flowers growing along the creek, picked a handful to make a bouquet and stuck them in the mud behind the log. At the right moment, I would reach back for them and hand them to Sharlene.

"Whatcha doing with those?" the kid asked.

"Making it look nice, that's all, so don't touch 'em."

"Okay."

I sat down on the log. It was a little dirty, but it would do. The wood footbridge shone brightly above in the late afternoon sun. I picked a long grass stem from the bank, put it between my teeth, and watched the stream forming little eddies. Water striders skidded across the surface with purpose in each stroke. Do they love? I wondered. The question startled me. Is that what we were—in love? What if this was all a big mistake?

Around that time, I had a recurring dream that I was being drawn irresistibly into a field of tall grass and flowers under a brilliant afternoon sun. Sharlene was there. There was nothing else but the wind fanning the grass and a queasiness in my stomach. Then, in the dream Sharlene and I would sit down and talk, and as I watched her mouth moving and her wavy blonde hair blowing in the wind, I would hear snickering through the grass, and the flowers would become heads with ogling eyes, and I would wake up.

It was a balmy spring day during recess when I asked Sharlene if she wanted to take a walk to the footbridge.

"To the footbridge? But we won't get back before the bell rings."

I shrugged.

"Why do you wanna go there?" she asked.

I shrugged again and smiled. "Just walking."

She was the sensible one and I the one on a major learning curve. The bridge would have to wait. I started thinking of some other way to get alone with her so that I could hold her hand and then kiss her. Finally I found my chance by circumstance rather than by planning. After school she normally took the bus home because she lived out of town, but one day she began walking away from school. I ran to catch up.

"Where ya going?"

"To my grandpa and grandma's house."

"Hey, they live by me. We can walk together."

"Okay," she said without breaking stride.

We had to cross the creek on a bridge a few blocks downstream from the footbridge. We paused, our hands side by side on the railing as we watched the creek below. We were unusually quiet. I threw a couple of stones, which made pock! sounds as they hit the water. I made sure my glasses were on straight before I reached over nonchalantly for Sharlene's hand. Just then she spoke.

"We'd better go. My grandparents are waiting."

"Yeah, I guess we better."

As we turned, I grazed her arm, and our hands became momentarily tangled. She squeezed my hand and playfully slapped it a few times. We walked on and my nerves settled. When we reached her grandparents' house, she said goodbye. I put my hands out to give her a hug. She resisted briefly, and then we hugged. Her blonde locks brushed my cheek. My heart rushed. When we pulled away, she looked shyly toward the house.

"Shall we walk to school together tomorrow?" I asked.

"I think my grandpa's walking with me tomorrow."

"Okay. Do you wanna take a walk to the footbridge on Saturday then?"

"Saturday? I think I'll be back home then," she said with a forced smile.

"Oh right."

I didn't like the look on her face. But for the moment we had made progress—a brush of hands and a brief hug—which in my mind was a brush with destiny. We had made contact, and who knew where this could go now? I certainly had no clue.

I continued to try to forge my destiny with Sharlene, anticipating my next move. In the meantime, I gave her things from my lunch that I knew she liked—chips and Milk Duds. I also gave her carefully crafted notes, clever ones that I'd worked on for several days—"You turn my multiplication tables into a multiple dessert table." And "You're the diamond in my baseball game and the swing in my homerun." Though I'd never hit one. She folded the notes and put them into her desk without a word and turned red. It appeared they were working.

Every Wednesday night, the members of our sixth grade had catechism class with Elder Vander Plaats. We were reviewing question number one in the Heidelberg Catechism: "What is your only comfort in life and death?"

My attention stopped on the word "death" because I had been feeling more death than life the past few days. Sharlene had been distant with me. Her smile was almost gone, even with my best jokes. We saw each other less and less at recess. I figured I'd said something stupid. Or maybe it was the walk to her grandparents' house and the hug. Was I being too bold? We were drifting back to the way things were before she'd arranged to sit behind me. I wondered if maybe she had tired of me and had started to see me simply as the dork in black glasses.

Elder Vander Plaats didn't get an immediate response and repeated the question, "Your only comfort in life and death?"

We mumbled the answer more or less in unison, quietly, lest anyone think we really meant what we were saying. "That I am not my own, but belong with body and soul, in life and in death, to my faithful Savior Jesus Christ."

"I am not my own" I could understand because I felt like I had lost control of myself, but this time, as we approached the end of the answer, I was absent-mindedly thinking "Sharlene" instead of "Jesus Christ" and startled myself. I quickly looked around. Had I actually said her name out loud? I looked Sharlene's way in the row ahead and several seats over. She was as pretty as ever, whispering to her friend and smiling. Her wavy blonde hair lay softly over her cheek.

Elder Vander Plaats was commentating on the answer with phrases like "the heavy price Jesus paid" and "his vicarious suffering" and "to have it any other way is idolatry."

I felt myself turn red. Was Sharlene my idol? Maybe this was the consequences of sin and selfishness.

That year Mr. Tjoelker taught us a term from our reading text that stuck in my mind—tragic irony. I remember it because what happened next was tragic and ironic—ironic because as with all blindsides I could never have seen coming what happened next, and tragic because, well, it was just tragic.

We were at the ball diamond at recess playing workup, and Jon Den Hartog, the brawniest, strongest kid in the class, was batting. Already at twelve his voice had dropped to the basement of base. He had the stoic face, square jaw, and thick dark hair of a boxer. He always chose the heaviest bat, and he could really put a hurt on the ball. When the next pitch came to him, he hurt it pretty badly, swatting it like a bug in a high arc over the bus garage into the blackberry brambles. It was majestic, and it wasn't his first homerun. He clobbered them like that on a regular basis.

Everyone, even the opposing team, stood in awe of the spectacle and cheered as Jon trotted the bases. As he rounded third base, I heard an especially loud scream above the others that I recognized. It was Sharlene. She was jumping up and down and clapping, her face pink with sheer joy. As Jon crossed home plate, he caught Sharlene's eye and smiled—the only smile I'd ever seen from him.

That was all I needed to be convinced Sharlene and I were done. She had traded in the scrawny kid with dark rimmed glasses for the biggest hitter in class—tragic irony. I should say "apparently we were done" because Sharlene never said anything about Jon. But I guess she didn't really have to.

In sixth grade, it was just the way things were. And who was I to argue with Jon Den Hartog? It was simply survival of the fittest, end of story.

The next day I saw Sharlene giving Jon's biceps a playful squeeze followed by a teasing sigh of amazement. Fair enough, all I had were jokes and answers to math problems. A few days after that, Sharlene ran up to me with a big smile, holding something out in her hand. A lump formed in my throat. I wondered if she had had a change of heart and was coming back to me. How would I handle such a reversal of fortune? On her finger she showed me a ring. It sparkled.

"Look. This is what Jon gave me," she said, gazing down at the ring.

"Oh," I said.

She turned and ran across the baseball diamond, her blonde locks bouncing up and down. It was her way of saying, "I'm with Jon now, sorry, but look how happy I am."

All this time, I had thought the key was holding her hand or giving her a kiss, while it was the ring all along—another irony. My face went hot. Had I made the wrong move, or was I just the wrong guy?

I concluded it wasn't anybody's fault. I was resigned to some mysterious law being played out, a law of attraction and repulsion that governed the molecules and movements of the spheres, a natural law that required no explanation because it was beyond the control of Sharlene, Jon, or me. It just was, and we simply obeyed it.

Whatever feelings I had about it I tried to ignore, my questions and grief left unspoken. The recurring dream of the summery field of windblown grass ceased to bless or trouble my sleep. Now that field was empty, no longer yellow with sun, the sky no longer endlessly blue but full of clouds with so many wispy, loose ends.

I was standing alone among the crowd of kids by the baseball diamond a couple of days later. Jon was walking up to home plate with a bat, and everyone was watching. I was expecting him to put an exclamation point on my loss of Sharlene when I felt someone from behind hook my arm and swing me around with a firm tug. It was Martin Walstra.

"Come here," he said.

I was puzzled. I didn't know Martin well, and I couldn't imagine what issue he might have with me. We walked.

Finally he said, "Jon stole Sharlene, didn't he?"

I was stunned. He had been following everything—my friendship with Sharlene, the ring, and Jon's takeover. Most everyone was aware, but Martin had taken my tragedy to heart, and here he was taking me into his confidence. The way he seemed to understand what I was feeling completely blindsided me. Sobs caught in my throat as I felt my grief for the first time.

"Did he ask if he could have her?" Martin asked, a rumble of anger in his voice.

"No," I said. "But I'm not mad at him."

"It doesn't matter, he can't do that." And then he added, "You're my buddy, okay?"

I nodded. At that moment Martin showed something I hadn't considered, that maybe I was wrong about the law of the universe that said the strongest must win. Maybe Jon and Sharlene were wrong. But also, maybe in the end nothing would change. The outcome didn't matter to me as much as the fact I knew someone cared and was on my side. I felt a strange sense of confidence.

"Don't worry," he said, looking to the sky, thinking. "Jon's a bully, and I'm going to beat the shit out of him." This was the biggest blindside of all.

After I'd taken in what he was saying, that he was actually going to challenge the wrong done, I told him to forget about it. I didn't want him to make a public scene, much less start a fight. And I was afraid for Martin. He was big but not a fighter. Jon could hurt him like he hurt a baseball.

The next day during morning recess, I noticed Jon and Martin squaring off inside a loose circle of boys on the gravel lot. The two of them were exchanging words, and others were egging them on. There was a shove from Jon, and I heard someone say Sharlene's name.

"What makes you think you can push your way around? Stay away from her," Martin was saying.

"She has my ring, so take off," Jon was saying. "Hear me?"

Jon had a point. Sharlene had accepted his ring, and whatever he had done to win her over, he'd done it well. But Martin didn't see it that way, as if he knew something I didn't.

"What's it to ya?" somebody shouted at Martin. "She wasn't your girlfriend, she was Karl's."

I shrank back into an invisible shell as Martin drew up into Jon's face. Jon didn't appear to want a fight. They stood like two boxers facing off, and Martin repeated the same thing he'd said to me. "I'm going to beat the shit out of you."

"You don't have a chance," Jon said. "You decide when."

A couple of guys urged them to get into it right then and there. The two stared at each other a bit longer until Jon finally turned away. Several of the guys followed Jon, each lobbying to be his fight manager, while Martin was left standing alone. I walked up to him. He was shaking.

"You told him off," I said. "That should be enough."

But the look on his face told me this was far from over. He was determined to fight Jon, and now he'd made it public. Nothing could change his mind. He hooked my arm and leaned against me as if he might crumple under the weight of his choice, the school's expectations on his shoulders, and now he needed *me* to support *him*.

Seldom had I seen the morale of the school so high as it was after the faceoff in the gravel lot. A fight was brewing between Martin and Jon, and it was only a question of when and where. I felt scared and responsible.

I saw Jon with his back against the school building, his hands in his pockets, and Sharlene was talking to him. She looked worried. What could I say to them? I could only make things worse. It was Friday, and I thought if we could just get through the day, maybe everything would blow over by Monday, and no one would care anymore, and no one would have to lift a finger to hit anyone. But that hope was short lived. Rumors were churning quickly, which I got wind of in the hallway when the bell rang for the end of lunch hour.

"It's this afternoon," someone whispered.

"After school?"

"No, at recess."

"Where?"

"Boys' bathroom."

Mr. Tjoelker complimented us on how quiet and well behaved we were for a Friday, failing to recognize the suppressed anxiousness in the room. No one wanted to give anything away, or Mr. Tjoelker would snuff out the fight immediately. And if I mentioned anything to try and stop it, I'd be beat up myself.

The bell rang for afternoon recess, and the guys made a quick exit. The girls didn't want to have anything to do with it and scooted outside. At the end of the hall, at the door to the boys' john, Rick and Neil were standing like sentries.

"It's reserved," Rick told a fifth grader, who turned and walked directly away.

The sixth grade guys were leaning against the walls, trying to pretend nothing was happening. I paced at the far end of the hall, hoping it would end quickly. Everyone was whispering about who was going to beat up who.

Just then Mr. Tjoelker poked his head into the hall.

"What's going on?" he asked.

"Nothin'," Eugene said. "We're just thinking about what to do for recess."

"While you're thinking, why don't a couple of you guys come and help me out."

Two guys quickly volunteered just to get Mr. Tjoelker preoccupied. I looked out the window at the end of the hall. From the second floor, I could see Sharlene waiting outside, glancing anxiously at the front door, probably waiting for Jon, hoping he wouldn't fight. The playground itself looked anxious. The baseball field was bare except for a few stray bats propped against the backstop and a ball waiting by the pitcher's mound. Blackberry brambles looped menacingly over the outfield fence. The shingles on the bus garage roof looked expectant, waiting to be lit up by another homerun.

Just then, Martin appeared and walked toward the bathroom while the guys parted like the Red Sea to let him through. Jon was already waiting for him inside. Everyone was trying to hear what was happening in the bathroom. Suddenly there was a loud thud against the wall, followed by a violent sound of flesh meeting flesh. There were a few grunts, and finally one long groan. Everything went quiet as we waited. Neil pushed the door open a crack to see inside and then backed away as Jon emerged, dabbing his right fist with a wet paper towel.

"Did you get him?" somebody asked.

Jon did not answer and headed down the stairs to the first floor, looking lonely and sad.

A couple of guys went in and came back out with their hands over their mouths. I forced my way through and found Martin in the corner of the bathroom, a crumpled heap. He was shaking, holding the side of his head, and blood was coming from his mouth. He sobbed, and my heart broke for him. I couldn't say anything. I was overwhelmed, seeing Martin so fragile and helpless.

"Don't worry," he said. "I'll be okay. It's done."

"Yeah, it's done" was all I could manage. I pushed up my glasses nervously.

Martin's left eye was swelling, but he wore a look of relief. A smile tried to force its way through the blood. "He got me good," he said.

Not a word was mentioned about the fight or what brought it on for the rest of the school year. For a couple of weeks, Martin's black eye and cut lip told the story. Everyone was awkward around Martin, as if they believed they themselves had beaten him up.

The number of school fights fell to almost none. Martin and Jon had done us all a favor by showing what the law of the jungle really meant if followed to its logical conclusion. On the surface the conclusion was obvious—Jon got Martin good.

But Martin got us all good by turning the law of the jungle on its head. Somewhere behind his swollen-shut eye, he saw the truth of the matter. Even though he'd lost the fight, and probably knew he would lose, at least for a moment he had overturned the law that I thought was irrefutable—the law that says the strongest win—because he'd shown us a greater law, the way of friendship and what it can cost to stand by a friend, that it meant being prepared to lose in order to win. He'd won me completely.

A year later, when I was in seventh grade and we were playing baseball, I saw a sixth grade kid at the adjacent diamond standing by himself. He was kicking at the ground while the rest of his class was playing. He'd got picked last and in protest decided not to play at all. I walked up to him and hooked his arm with mine, and a question jumped spontaneously out of my mouth.

"Hey . . . what's your only comfort in life and death?"

He just stared at me and wrinkled his forehead. The question surprised me too and made me laugh.

"Even if you're picked last, you still have to belong to somebody," I said. "You gotta have a buddy."

I led him to our ball diamond, where Jon was getting ready to cream another one over the bus garage.

"Watch this," I told him.

Chapter 13

Shit

We first noticed the blackouts when Mom suddenly stopped slicing the meatloaf and stood staring into the dining room, where we were sitting down for dinner.

"Need a hand, Mom?" Nancy asked.

Mom gazed into the distance a moment longer. "What did you say?"

"Did you forget something?"

"Why, isn't this enough? I've already got potatoes, beans, and meatloaf."

"You were just staring."

"Well, forget about it. Somebody take this to the table."

We looked at each other, Dad at Mom, and chuckled. The staring episode was forgotten as a momentary loss of concentration until it happened again a few days later. Dale found her in the middle of the family room staring off toward the garden. When she came out of it, she asked if anyone had picked up milk. How long she'd been standing there was anybody's guess.

"I just lost my train of thought there for a minute," she said.

Somebody casually mentioned dementia one day, but Mom was only forty-seven and at the top of her game. She was feeling a new lease on life with her youngest finally in school and the rest of us also preoccupied. Sharon, Don, and Shirley were not living at home. Dale and Nancy were in high school, and Ken and I were in elementary school all day along with Keith. That meant Mom was free. She had finished a teaching degree, got married, had eight kids, and now she was finally in the classroom doing what she'd trained for. She could get out of the house where she'd been homemaker for over twenty years, go to women's functions more often, and spend more time in the garden. She walked to her fourth grade class every morning, smiling with her face to the sky.

On Saturday, with her marking done, she sat in the study writing Sharon a letter to tell her about the "new phase" in her life. Halfway through the letter, her sentence started trailing below the line and off the page. She had blacked out again.

"Oh, my lands, look at this. I've never done that before." She held up her letter to Dad. "It's all crooked."

Dad looked, and the rest of us cocked our heads at the drooping line.

"Wouldya ever," she said. "I'll have to start all over."

"Don't worry, you can fix it," someone said. "Look, on this line just scratch out 'yesterday afternoon in the garden' and start a new line with it here, and you're fine. Sharon's not going to care."

But Mom cared. She took out a fresh piece of stationary and started over, and her frustration grew when it happened again.

"What am I doing here!" she cried. "I can't make heads or tails of this."

Dad took another look. The letter started comprehensible but became nonsensical as her sentence trailed off into a jumble of words corresponding to nothing. Mom ripped the page into pieces and held her head in her hands, confused and scared.

"What's happening to me?"

"We'll go to the doctor Monday and see what they say," Dad said.

The doctor referred her to a neurologist. She and Dad drove to Seattle, where they did some tests. Her X-rays came back showing a mass in her frontal lobe the size of a small peach pit. It was putting pressure on the part of her brain that controlled her cognitive abilities, like language. The doctor said the blackouts were actually little seizures. They would continue, possibly get worse, if the tumor wasn't removed.

Mom sat in shock. Dad paused before asking the question no husband and father of eight would ever want to utter. "Is it cancer?"

"There's no way of telling until we get in there, take it out, and take a sample of it for testing."

"So it could be," Dad said, his voice weakening. "How dangerous is it—the surgery?"

"There's always risk."

"Risk?"

"Depending how hard it is to remove the tumor. If it's tangled, it could mean we either leave it in or risk permanent damage to Irene's cognitive skills. Or risk death in rare cases if she reacts negatively to the anesthesia . . . or after surgery if . . . "

Mom looked on, wondering if the doctor was talking about someone else. The doctor asked whether they had saved the letters Mom was writing during her seizures so that he could have a look at them. They might offer some valuable data to his research.

Mom spoke for the first time. "No, I ripped them up and threw them away!" she said definitively, as if leveling a verdict on the offending mass in her brain.

Dad wanted to ask how many of his patients had encountered the risk factors he mentioned, like dying for example, but the doctor was already giving instructions about scheduling surgery, making necessary preparations, and signing forms.

Mom picked up her purse. "Come on, Pete, let's go."

The day came soon for Mom's brain surgery. To make things easier, The Three K's were sent to live with friends in the church. Vander Meys across the street took Keith in, and Ken and I shipped off to Vermeers, who were on a farm less than a mile out of town. It would be a good long walk to school. Dale and Nancy would fare just fine at home with Dad when Dad wasn't in Seattle with Mom.

"It will be fun," Dad assured Ken and me. "Vermeers have two boys and a dog, and you'll get to live on a farm and see where our milk comes from. You'll have to help out though. I told them to put you to work."

Dad and Mom chose not to tell us three youngest about the risks Mom would be facing and never mentioned the C-word to protect us from the possibility of deep loss. We were meant to see this as a brief interruption, an adventure of sorts. We only knew that Mom "needed to have a tumor removed from her forehead." But by Dad's tone I sensed Mom was going into greater danger than what was implied by simply a visit to the farm. And if Dad didn't dare mention it, neither did I want to imagine it. Instead, the unspoken threat ebbed and flowed amorphously like the tide, in swells of anxiety and undertows of denial.

Our stay on the farm was a mixed bag. The idea of having a couple playmates during our time there was short-lived. The Vermeer boys were older and out of school, busy helping their dad with the milking. Mrs. Vermeer loved having "two young ones" in the house. She showed us some toys she'd kept from her boys' younger days. Most impressive was a bucket of plastic soldiers, which Ken and I quickly dug into, arranging them into huge battle alignments over the living room floor and waging war like opposing generals. At one point, our battle came to a pitch and Ken told me to "shut up" as Mrs. Vermeer appeared from the kitchen.

"Kenneth, we don't talk that way. I don't want to hear that word again, alright?"

Ken nodded. The second day, we were put to work in the barn, as Dad had promised, but getting up in the dark to work was more than we'd bargained for. Mr. Vermeer and his sons teased us that they'd been up for two hours already milking the cows, and it was time we got our grubs on.

"We're going to get you guys out to do some cleaning up," Mr. Vermeer said, rolling a cigarette. "The Mrs. will find ya some boots."

He lit his cigarette and headed out the door while Mrs. Vermeer found us each a pair of rubber boots, a couple sizes too large. She giggled as she watched us walk out to the barn with Neal, their youngest son. He didn't seem to be as excited about taking care of us as his mom was.

"Got you some shit kickers there?" he said, grinning, as we flopped and clopped, trying to keep up with his long strides across the yard to the barn.

As we stepped into the barn, Neal asked louder than was necessary, "Who wants to scrape shit?" Before we could answer, he was handing us each a long-handled tool with a wide blade at the business end.

Our job was to scrape the cow manure off the central aisle of the barn into the gutters on either side. Then Neal followed after us with the wheelbarrow, shoveling the manure out the gutters.

Neal said, "My mom's got cinnamon buns when we're done scraping."

He seemed to have had more than enough of the farm. He worked quickly, as though he smelled cinnamon buns above the stench of manure. He grunted and stewed and heaved, then stormed out of the barn with a full wheelbarrow, muttering under his breath, and dumped his load into the manure spreader, or "shit wagon."

Ken said, "How come she chews me out for saying 'shut up' but Neal says the S-word all the time?"

"You mean 'sugar'?" I said.

"No. 'Shit.'"

"You just said it."

"No, I didn't."

"Yes, you did."

"It doesn't count because I'm just telling you want he said, so shut up."

"Kenneth, we don't talk that way."

Ken held his scraper up like he wanted to hit me. Neal came back with an empty wheelbarrow and stopped suddenly when he saw that I was scraping manure into the gutter he'd just shoveled clean.

"Not in there, ya dumb shit, I just cleaned that! Scrape it to the other side!"

"That's Ken's side."

"Well, now it's your side."

He shoveled the gutter clean again and moved over to Ken's side to do that gutter. When he was done, he asked Ken if he wanted to help him take the load out. "We have to spread it in the field. I'll let you drive the tractor."

He said it loud enough to make sure I knew I wasn't welcomed. Neal was dumb. I didn't want to go out with him on some stupid tractor anyway. Why was he so grumpy about a little manure? *His* mom wasn't in the hospital, was she? *She* didn't have to get a tumor taken out of her head, and he didn't have to go live at a strange place for two whole weeks. I heard the tractor start up, and I went to the house to change my clothes for school.

The best part of staying on the farm was Sunday when Mrs. Vermeer served banana cream and coconut cream pie, which she'd made on Saturday rather than on the Lord's Day, when no unnecessary work was to be done, especially when done for pleasure alone. On Sunday we also had the entire afternoon to play on the living room floor with the plastic toy soldiers while Mr. Vermeer took a long nap in his recliner. This worked out as long as we didn't nudge his feet, which would earn us a reflex kick in our backs.

One afternoon a few days into our stay, we heard Mrs. Vermeer on the phone, engaged in a serious conversation. After she hung up, she came to Ken and me with news about Mom. Mom had come through the surgery and seemed to be doing very well. Ken took this as a matter of fact—of course she was going to be fine. She was our mom. I felt my anxiety subside. The tide was going out. But we would be sticking around a little longer, Mrs Vermeer said with a smile, because our mom would have to stay in the hospital just a few more days.

The next day Ken and I walked down Vermeer's lane on our way to school.

"Did you change your clothes?" I asked Ken.

"Yeah, did you?"

"Yeah, but I still smell it. Smell your hands."

REFORMED

The smell of manure was hard to get rid of. It was everywhere—in the fields, in the air, in the barn and house, sometimes even in fresh clothes. Some days, if the wind was right, you could even smell it in town. Hygienists who visited our class would emphasize the importance of not only brushing teeth and hair but also using a toothbrush to get under the fingernails. Everyone knew the hygienist meant getting the cow manure out. It could get stuck under fingernails for days. She also emphasized washing our hands several times a day. Having spent only a few days on the farm, I now understood why the creases in farmers' hands were often brown.

"My hands smell like shit!" I said.

"Better not say that in front of Mom and Dad."

"Say what?"

"That word you said." Ken wasn't falling for my bait.

The use of unrefined language was one of many contradictions about my religious upbringing. The language of the barn was not the language of the church. On the farm, words like "shit" were commonplace, but you'd never hear the word uttered at a church gathering. I would look back later, wondering how people managed to scrape the Bible clean of its vulgarities—like the shit-stained barn where Jesus was born to the cross he was nailed to, from the mud Adam was made of to the prophets' public nakedness, from Cain killing Able to murders by God's chosen people. The Bible was filled with unseemly details, but some people just wouldn't allow the barn into church or, conversely, let God into the barn.

By the second Sunday, the Vermeer boys were complaining about having to constantly step through our war games sprawled across the living room, and I was getting homesick. We were feeling like we'd had enough of our farm visit when a call came from Dad that Mom was coming home from the hospital. Mrs. Vermeer served us hamburgers and fries that night for supper, and Mr. Vermeer drove us home.

We were waiting at the house while Dad was on the way home with Mom from Seattle. When the door finally opened, there was Mom, walking very gingerly on Dad's arm. Dale, Nancy, Ken, Keith, and I gathered as Dad lowered Mom slowly into an armchair. He announced that the tumor was benign.

"That's good news," Dale said.

"What does 'be nine' mean?" I asked.

"No cancer," Nancy said jubilantly.

SHIT

Dad had bought Mom a wig to cover her shaved head though it didn't look right on her. It was too dark and was missing curls. She grinned sheepishly, modeling her new look, as we solemnly took in the mom who had been taken from us and had come back with someone else's hair. Her lip quivered.

"I'm just happy to be with my family," she said.

"We're very relieved and thankful," Dad said, speaking for all of us.

Mom asked, "Do you want to see it?"

Everyone did. She ceremoniously removed her wig to reveal a mom I'd never seen before.

"Here I am," she said.

Her bald scalp was a map of wrinkles and blood vessels. She pointed to the incision on her forehead where the surgeon had to open her skull. We stared in silence. Keith leaned in, propping himself on Mom's knees. I couldn't help grimacing. A red L-shaped line ran three inches down her forehead and took an abrupt turn three inches right, like the flap door of a pup tent, where the tumor had come out and the flap zipped shut again.

Thanksgiving Day fell on the same week that Mom came home. In the church service, we sang the hymn "Praise God From Whom All Blessings Flow" as though singing it for the first time. A couple of women from the church brought over turkey, yams, and stuffing, more than we could eat. Dad gave an extra long prayer before our generously provided Thanksgiving dinner. We didn't need to go around the table that year saying what we were most thankful for. Mom's blackouts had stopped, the shit had been cleaned out, and our mom was back.

— Chapter 14 —

Canadian League

I was eleven when I played my first little league baseball game. We were the visiting team against the best team in our division, a Canadian team in Ladner, British Columbia, in a cross-border match up. I was playing shortstop. The first pitch was hit directly to me, a routine ground ball. I was on it in perfect position when the ball took a crazy hop and hit me flush in the mouth. The runner was safe at first, the home crowd cheered, and some laughed at the on-field comedy provided by the visiting team.

The game stopped. Coach Bradley ran out onto the field to check me out. With tears in my eyes and blood seeping from a cut lip, I nodded that I was okay. He said I should come out of the game, but I shook my head. I didn't want to give the crowd a closer look at me and hear them laughing again. Coach knew what was going on and let me stay on the field. When we got to the bench, I was feeling a bit woozy, and Coach told two teammates to go sit with me and give me some cheering up. A couple of the guys gave me pats on the back and assured me it was just a little cut, but the way they screwed up their faces said otherwise. My pride was wounded far more than my mouth.

After that embarrassing episode, I understood the pressures a live audience could impose. Another day would come when I was reminded of the burden of being the spectacle of a painful moment. It came one day when a friend and I had a rare chance to go to Nat Bailey stadium in Vancouver for a professional minor league baseball game between the Vancouver home team and visiting Portland.

It was a pitchers' duel with very little hitting. To keep things interesting, the stadium officials offered live entertainment between innings, designed as advertising for the team's various sponsors. One major sponsor was White Spot, a family restaurant chain founded by Nat Bailey himself, who also happened to be a huge baseball fan and a big time donor. The name White Spot was a mystery to me. It seemed an unfortunate name for a restaurant, conjuring visions of white spots on food. Hey, how about a White Spot burger with fries? It would give you pause.

That day, in the lull between the fifth and sixth innings, White Spot was providing one lucky fan the chance to beat the clock and win lunch for four at one of their restaurants. A kid was pulled from the stands and handed several placards with giant letters on them, which would spell "White Spot" when unscrambled and laid out in the correct order. The contestant this day was ten-year-old Cindy.

She stood confidently in the batter's warm-up circle, her frail frame nearly eclipsed by the large placards. She was on the clock.

"You have one minute!" came the announcement over the loudspeakers. "Cindy, are you ready?"

She nodded vigorously, and the bell rang. She was off, skipping back and forth along the third base line, slapping down letters faster than a short order burger cook. The announcer did the play-by-play while the crowd cheered Cindy on, which only made her nervous. With thirty seconds left, she had placed down all the letters but two—the "W," which she held in her hand, and the "E," which she did not see lying face down behind her.

"Twenty seconds," the announcer urged.

Overcome by the moment, Cindy danced unsteadily, with the crowd shouting, some laughing, "No! No! The other way!"

Cindy looked up to the stands bewildered and held out her hands for help. She had spelled out neatly along the third base line, "S-H-I-T" and "P-O-T," but couldn't see what was wrong or how to fix it.

"Switch out the 'S'!"

"The 'W'! It's in your hand, the 'E' is right there on the ground!"

With everyone screaming at once, Cindy grew even more flustered. She hopped from one foot to the other, her long locks flipping back and forth, the "W" still clinging to her hand.

The bell sounded before Cindy realized she had been holding the all-important first letter all along. Embarrassed but smiling like a good sport, Cindy shuffled back to her seat in the stands, leaving the offending words still sprawled out on the field, an advertisement gone awry for the home team's primary sponsor, while fans shouted their mock disapproval. An usher rushed out and awkwardly gathered up the placards.

I'd blown it on the field and suffered derision too. I knew how Cindy felt.

Mr. Bradley was the first coach I'd had for anything. He was short but athletic, a blue collar guy. He always came to practice in his forest green work clothes—slightly baggy pants and a shirt with the logo of the auto body shop where he worked. He must have liked green because he ordered us green t-shirts with our team name, Wolves, written across them in yellow cursive lettering. We were proud and hungry. He looked at us with contemplation and doubt in his round face, the sun reflecting off his bald head, wondering what stuff his Wolves were made of.

I admired Coach Bradley. No matter how hard players complained, he was fair and stuck to his decisions. He explained that he wanted honesty, hard play, and good sportsmanship, which was hard to find in a group of eleven- and twelve-year-olds who felt the need to assert themselves.

I was nervous at our first practice. The guys all knew each other, but I didn't know anybody. They were classmates at the public school, and I was coming over from the Christian school. Coach understood what it took for me to leave my comfort zone and blend in with a group of strangers. He tried to make me feel part of the group and made sure everyone knew I was no different than the rest of them.

Coach had a hard time getting our Sumas team into a little league division because Sumas was so far out in the sticks, even for the closest teams, so other teams didn't want to bus our way. But Coach was determined, so he did some cross-border shopping and got hold of the little league organization in Canada. This was out of the ordinary, but they were nice enough to let us into their league. Most of the teams were no more than twenty minutes away, and they were eager to play a real American baseball team.

Our cross-border skirmishes became games of legend . . . for the Canadian teams. Each one welcomed us, eager to beat us up, which they did pretty badly. Coach clapped for us regardless after every game, not willing to give in to self-pity or wounded pride, and told us, "We'll get 'em next time." He wanted only to make sure we were having fun, which we were when we managed to forget about the lopsided scores. It didn't help that the Canadian teams had not only shirts but whole uniforms, including pants and cleats. We had to admit they were impressive. There was a "mercy rule," which Coach invoked often, for when the score differential was more than twelve runs by the fifth inning. He'd wave his hat and tell the other coach he had to get his guys home for supper.

He was like a dad to some of the guys who came from broken homes and had seldom felt a dad's presence. He had his hands full with a few exuberant but troubled kids.

Our third baseman, Manny, some thought was a foster kid because he was brown skinned, while his parents were marshmallow white. I liked him. He could make me laugh. When we first met, I thought he was the exact embodiment of the cartoon character Goofy because he flopped around like Goofy when he talked, always joking and laughing.

Coach Bradley put Manny at third base because that floppy arm of his was a slingshot. He whipped the ball across the diamond, and it would be on the first baseman quicker than twelve boys on a watermelon in July. The pitcher heard the ball *whiz* past his ear on the way to Phil at first base as Phil stuck his mitt out in front of his face, cringing at the anticipated sting of the ball. He took his mitt off each time he caught Manny's ball to shake the bees out of his hand and hollered, "Not so damn hard!"

Coach gave Phil some extra padding to put on the inside of his glove and told him he was just going to have to get used to it, showing him how he could absorb the force of the ball so it wouldn't hurt so much.

With Manny's slingshot arm also came a few wild throws. He would overthrow first base, chuckle, flop around, and look sheepish, as the runner rounded first on the way to second. After a few overthrows, some of the guys started giving him the raspberries.

"Come on! Hit the target!" they yelled, throwing their mitts to the ground with the runner on his way to third base.

Manny was not the only one making mistakes though. Everyone did but assumed it was only the other players who screwed up. As mistakes mounted, the yelling got louder.

"You're throwing like a girl!"

"Come on! Get the lead out!"

Coach saw a teachable moment, stopped play, and called the team in.

"There's one rule you have to learn," he said. "There will be no chewing each other out. If anyone needs chewing out, I'll do it." Zeek, our catcher, took the bubble gum from his mouth and dropped it to the ground. Coach stared down each player, making a couple of us repeat what he'd just said until he was sure we'd got it.

"Now, who was playing right field?" he asked.

Greg raised his hand.

"Okay, where were you on that overthrow to first base?"

Greg shrugged. "Right field?"

Coach showed us what backing each other up looked like, positioning himself at various spots on the field behind each play in question.

"The right fielder's job on a throw from third to first," he hollered, "is to back up first base like this." He ran up behind first base. "A ball hit to shortstop or second base is backed up by the center fielder." He ran behind second base. "Like this. On a ball hit to third," he said panting, "shortstop goes over . . . like this . . . behind third." Coach was just getting warmed up. "Okay, what about a rundown? When you've got the runner in a pickle between first and second . . ." He paused and called three guys over and made one of them the runner to help him demonstrate. "Okay, I'm the second baseman over here. I chase the runner back to first like this. Now run back," he instructed the runner. "When he turns back to first, I throw to first. The first baseman chases him back to second, the shortstop takes my place at second, and I go behind the first baseman at first . . . like this. First baseman throws it to second . . . and then goes behind the shortstop . . . the shortstop throws it to me at first and comes in behind me, and so on . . ." Coach stopped, leaning over to catch his breath, and went down on one knee. "Until the runner gets tired . . , and you tag him. Go ahead," he said laughing, "tag me."

Coach called us around him as he was down on all fours sucking in air. "That's called . . . backing each other up. And all the time, I'm on the bench watching how you guys are working together. And hoping you make accurate throws." He climbed back to his feet. "You got it?"

No one said anything because no one really did get it and didn't want to be called on to demonstrate again.

"You gotta lay yourselves out there for each other, okay? Don't chew out your teammate, put out the runner. Put out, don't chew out. And back each other up." He told us to repeat the last thing he said and then pointed us to various places to practice rundowns and backing each other up.

At the end of training week, Coach Bradley announced our positions for the first game. He said I would be playing shortstop. Several guys groaned with envy. It was the most coveted position on the field because so many balls were hit between second and third. I felt honored. There were guys with stronger arms, but Coach liked how I got down on the ball and got rid of it quickly. He'd paused once during ground ball practice and singled me out to say, "There, that's how it's done, good transfer, did you guys see that?" He hit another hot one to me. I fielded it cleanly and threw to first. "See that?"

I thought Coach may have seen a bit of himself in me. Like him, I was small, and he had the no-nonsense attitude of someone who knew what it meant to be an outsider himself.

After practice one day, Coach Bradley overheard a couple of the guys mumbling about why the "little Christian kid" got to play shortstop. Coach Bradley was not a churched man, but he sat the two down, gave them a good chewing out, and wouldn't let them play until they convinced him he would never hear comments like that again about anyone. They never said anything else about my faith or my size. The pressure was on me to prove I could play shortstop, and I did.

We lost our first game against Ladner, 12-1, our only run coming on a throwing error. My lip healed over the next couple weeks while I continued playing. But after that first game, it was all downhill as far as proving we belonged in the Canadian league. We didn't win one game the whole season, which was a real kick in the pants for us Americans. We'd invented the game, for Pete's sake, so we figured we should have had the inside edge, but Coach would never listen to any moaning or excuses.

As a final word, he announced to the team with as much positivity as he could muster, "We all had a good time." He told us we could keep our shirts. We glanced at each other and grinned.

"We learned a lot . . ." He said, thought for a moment, and continued as if trying to convince himself, ". . . learned a lot about humility and backing each other up. That's the most important thing." He led us in a final cheer of hip hip hooray, which we had done after every game. We were fresh young shoots in our green uniforms, blending with the infield grass that had begun to turn us from boys to men.

— Chapter 15 —

Aunt Jemima

After his first season, Coach Bradley decided against coaching again, which left me at a loss about what to do with my summer. Ken and I were soft-tossing a baseball with Fred and Rodney one afternoon, and we looked up when a stubble-faced man with arms as thick as tree stumps stepped out of his pickup and came toward our circle.

Before he'd even reached us, he was asking, "Any of you hardy lads wanna work? Make some money?" He talked with a lisp that didn't match his deep, resonant voice.

We looked at each other. "Doing what?"

"Picking berries. Strawberries first. We'll see how that goes, then maybe raspberries." He spat a brown streak to one side.

We shrugged. Rodney walked away.

"I don't know," Fred said.

"You don't wanna make lotsa money?" he asked Fred.

"Nah, not really."

"What about you guys?" he asked Ken and me. "Do you like money?"

"Sure."

"Where do you guys live?"

I pointed to our house across the street.

"The preacher's kids?"

We nodded.

"How about it? I have a lot of kids picking for me from around Sumas. Some of them make three, four hundred dollars a summer. I'll come with my bus and pick you up in front of your house and drop you off at the end of the day." It sounded like he'd used this sales pitch a few times.

The sound of so much money got our attention though we had no idea what it would cost us in return. The man introduced himself as Darryl. He followed us across the street so he could talk to our dad and mom.

The offer really fed Dad's work ethic. He couldn't have been more delighted about getting us into the berry fields and trained in some manual labor. Getting our hands dirty and learning how to make some money, he figured, would be the best thing for us.

"Sure, our boys can work. They do our garden every year, so I think they can work the fields." He pointed a thumb to our garden, cleaned of weeds the day before, which was getting a good douse from the water sprinkler.

"Looks better than my fields," Darryl said loudly and let out a falsetto, tee-hee laugh, revealing warmth beneath his tough exterior.

Darryl picked us up as promised Monday morning, a sunny day in June. His yellow school bus was already half full of pickers from around town. Twenty minutes later we were at the strawberry fields. Darryl directed us to a tangled pile of triangle-shaped metal buggies, small low-riding wheelbarrows, and told us to select one. On the buggy, we fit a wood flat of a dozen boxes, six inches square. The field boss assigned us a row, one person on each side, and showed us how to find the berries by lifting the bushes while kneeling in the dirt.

Ken and I looked down our row and then sideways across the forty acres of strawberries, row on row. Heat shimmered off the field in waves already at 8:30am. The end of our row seemed a mile away. The task seemed daunting. In the bushes, clusters of red plump berries drooped under their own weight. Three of them could barely fit in my hand. We weren't supposed to eat the berries, but few kids could resist. The juice oozed down our chins, a mouthful of summer sun and rain. A couple kids ate so many they got sick and threw up. Darryl laughed like he'd seen it a hundred times. His tee-hee-hee sailed over the field.

"Tomorrow's a new day!" he encouraged the sick ones. "Look at the bright side. After this, the only place you'll want to put those berries is in your flat."

Even when he had to send us back down our rows to pick the berries we missed, he chatted us up with a joke or a story to keep up our morale, but he was usually the only one laughing.

At Darryl's shrill whistle, we stopped to eat our bag lunches in the shade of tall Douglas Firs bordering the field, and after we'd regained some energy, we headed back to our rows. By mid-afternoon, Ken and I had each picked about six flats. We carried them to the checkers to get scrutinized for rotten or green berries, and the checker punched a hole in a card pinned to our chests—one flat, one punch, seventy-five cents earned. By 4:00 we had each made about five dollars.

We came home with sore knees and backs, strawberry stains on our pants, hands, faces, and in our hair, which stiffened straight out from our heads until Mom couldn't recognize us. As the days wore on, the fields got hotter and more miserable. Finally, we got a string of rainy days. Then our hands got so cold we couldn't feel the berries. Darryl wouldn't shut down work because of rain unless there was no let up on the horizon.

The Native migrant workers were picking before we arrived and were still picking when Darryl drove us home. I couldn't see how they did it. I was aching, sticky, and tired already by noon. After the first week, on the bus ride home, I wanted more than anything to find Coach Bradley to get the baseball team back together again so I wouldn't have to pick anymore.

After a few days kids got bored picking and started berry fights. A berry came whizzing by my head, and I looked up to see one kid, who pretended he hadn't thrown it. I flung one back. Other kids who were caught in the crossfire started throwing too, and soon the juicy red bullets were creating crosshatch patterns over the berry field.

Some people brought their transistor radios from home and played top forty music to take the edge off the heat, which resulted in competing music coming from different stations. One kid would be playing "Yummy, Yummy, Yummy," while another played "Jumpin' Jack Flash" just to drown him out. One girl made the mistake of playing "Strawberry Fields Forever," and everyone started pelting her with strawberries.

"Turn that stupid song off! We don't need to be reminded."

Even the Beatles could sound more like mockery than music in the heat of a strawberry patch.

For bathrooms, Darryl had wooden outhouses set up at intervals around the field. Once, another picker I hardly knew came hurdling over the rows toward me.

"Hey, Jeffrey's in the crapper," he told me. "Let's tip him."

Together we put our hands on the side of the outhouse, and started it rocking.

Jeffrey called from inside, "Hey, I'm in here!"

"Who's *I'm*?"

The outhouse teetered, hung for a moment on its edge, and tipped onto its side. We heard a thud and Jeffrey's howls from inside. The hole in the ground exposed two weeks' worth of waste from pickers, checkers, and field bosses. The stench filtered into the air. The door budged, a head appeared, and Jeffrey crawled out, pulling up his pants. Darryl had apparently seen this one a few times too. He didn't even ask who'd knocked it over and grabbed a couple guys nearby to right the outhouse.

Later that day, as I pushed my cart forward in the row, I felt a thwack in the back of my head and felt a wad of strawberry in my hair. I turned to see a girl two rows over with her head in the bushes, giggling. She looked up, biting into a strawberry, then scooted her cart up to sit even with me.

"What happened to your head?"

She was cute and chatty. Her name was Peggy Allen. We talked for most of the afternoon, ignoring how much pay we were losing by not picking, and moved no more than a few feet up our rows. She was welcome company in the midst of strawberry misery. After my thing with Sharlene, I knew I shouldn't jump to any conclusions that Peggy really liked me, but I also didn't want to blow a chance by being too slow on the uptake like last time. I decided to act boldly and forcefully and let the chips fall where they may. The radio after all was calling this "the summer of love," and anything could happen. Before the day was done, I asked her if she wanted to meet me in the park on Saturday at noon for a picnic. She giggled and nodded okay.

I wasn't good at making sandwiches, and I didn't want to ask Mom, so I bought some picnic items at Reitkirk's—a bag of chips, a choice of black and red licorice, and a couple of cans of pop. I was five minutes early and waited in the picnic shelter, where it was shaded, so I could be inconspicuous. I'd brought a blanket, which we could spread out in the grass along the creek.

Five minutes passed, then ten and fifteen, and no Patty. I was trying to assume the best—maybe she just wasn't as punctual as this Dutch boy. It dawned on me then that my parents wouldn't be too excited if Peggy ever came over to the house to see me. She wasn't from our church, maybe not from any church. I could never introduce her to my friends either without starting rumors about the preacher's kid and his heathen girlfriend. We would have to remain secret, like Romeo and Juliet.

After half an hour, I was wondering where my act of boldness had got me. The feelings of Sharlene's rejection came flooding back. Whatever it took in this business of romance, I obviously didn't have it. I left the park with my paper bag of picnic items, but rather than turning toward home, I turned toward Peggy's house. She'd told me where she lived.

Her house was a small shoebox of a place, badly in need of paint. Spindly weeds sprung up from bare ground in the yard. I took two steps up to the front door. The landing at the top of the steps had a long crack in its concrete surface. I knocked. The door opened and her mother eyed me from inside.

"Is Peggy home?" I asked through the screen door.

"Peggy, there's a boy here for you!"

"A what?" Peggy's voice came from deep inside the house.

"A *boy*!"

Peggy came outside to hang out on their desert of a yard as her mom watched from behind the screen door. Peggy was much more demure than she had been in the berry patch.

"Oh, the picnic, I forgot," she said, trying to smile. "I don't really like picnics that much."

"So you want to do something else then? Wanna play tennis?"

"No, I haven't got a racket," she said and turned to the house, and I thought I heard her giggle to herself. She glanced over her shoulder to say bye.

I didn't see Peggy in the berry fields again. A lot of kids couldn't stick it out for the entire season. Peggy had lasted a day. It was a brutal job, and not everyone was cursed with the Dutch work ethic. The end of strawberry season didn't come soon enough, after three weeks of sunburn, cracked hands, calloused knees, and disillusionment, just shy of a girlfriend and seventy-five dollars.

"Did someone make 400 dollars?" I asked one of the field bosses on the last day.

She laughed and asked where I'd heard that. I told her Darryl told us the day he hired us. She shook her head. "He must have meant the top pickers, who go on to pick raspberries too. That's the only way anyone around here makes 400 dollars. You get a dollar twenty-five a flat picking raspberries."

I looked beyond the strawberry fields to the tall canes of raspberries in the next field—400 dollars seemed out of reach. I was feeling done for the summer. The extracurricular activities had been memorable, but the picking was for the birds.

At home Dad asked Ken and me why we didn't want to pick raspberries. Obviously, he hadn't picked berries before. Then Nancy piped up that a raspberry farm east of town was desperate for pickers. She said she'd help us, and if it was too hard, we could quit.

"You get shade from the bushes and you don't have to crouch, you can stand up. The money's way better than strawberries. The owner is nice. She's a lady—Mrs. Witherspoon."

"Does she eat with a withered spoon?" I asked, and Ken laughed.

We finally gave in to the idea, prospectors chasing a dream, and Nancy drove us out to Witherspoon's to start our new jobs in raspberries. We were a little under aged and under height, so the deal was Nancy would have to supervise us. She showed us how to part the prickly canes to get at the berries without getting poked terribly, but scratches up and down the arms were a constant part of the job. By the end of the first week, Nancy complained to Mom that keeping us up to speed was more than she'd signed up for and said she wanted out of the arrangement and wanted to babysit instead. So, our house turned into a daycare of five or six kids at a time, while Ken and I would have to keep picking because we'd just be in the way if we stayed home.

With a little pressure from Dad, Mrs. Witherspoon agreed to keep us on without Nancy's oversight, but she put us under the close scrutiny of a field boss. We never knew our field boss's name. She didn't seem to want anyone to know. We called her Aunt Jemima because she was a spitting image of the Aunt Jemima on the pancake syrup bottle if you replaced the do-rag with a sun bonnet. And this Aunt Jemima was white not black, though you'd look twice on account of her dark skin tone from many hours under the sun.

We soon came to find that our Aunt Jemima was a far cry from the winsome face on the pancake syrup bottle. Our Jemima smoked on her breaks, leaning against a post at the end of a row. I couldn't imagine the original Aunt Jemima holding a cigarette in her mouth the way our field boss did like it was a little white stickperson dangling from her lips ready to commit suicide. Our Aunt Jemima never smiled, unlike the woman with the imperishable smile on the syrup bottle. She was cold and critical. The only time she ever talked was when she had something to complain about.

No matter how hard we worked, there was always something wrong with what we were doing.

"You're missing berries. Go back to where I marked it and start picking from there," she'd say.

We'd wander back until we found her mark. We'd look up the row to where we'd been, sigh, and repeat what we'd just done. That summer, "Here Comes the Judge" hit the singles charts, and whenever Ken or I saw Aunt Jemima coming down our row toward us, we started chanting, "here come da judge," just like in the song, as a warning to look busy.

It was Ken's birthday. I had argued the day should not be a work day because we should be celebrating, but Dad said we should treat the day like any other, that we had no birthday plans anyway. We could do something special after our work was done. It was a hot day without a breath of air. We were re-picking the same row for the second time when I heard Ken chanting, "here come da judge." And as usual, there she came in her sun bonnet, along with her gavel and her familiar sentence.

"Boys, go back over your row."

"We are already."

"Well, go back again."

"It's so hot the berries must be ripening behind us," Ken protested.

"Go back and clean it up. See this?" She held out a handful of berries she'd picked from our row, none of them ripe, and instead of dropping them into our boxes to go toward our credit like other berry bosses did, she picked up a sour orange one in her tobacco-charred lips and walked away.

"She's tormenting us," I said, "on purpose."

We could find only a smattering of raspberries we'd missed. I searched my memory for a word I'd heard from my teacher.

"Aunt Jemima's our oppressor."

"She's a *tyrant*," Ken said.

"She probably makes her kids eat raspberries with dirt for every meal. She probably doesn't even have kids or she'd know they'd get fed up and turn on her."

We picked fast to get done with our row and ran to get assigned a new one before Aunt Jemima could return and make us go back again. Unfortunately, it didn't get past her scrutinizing eyes. She dragged us off our new row back to the old one to re-pick it a third time. Since our wages depended on how much we picked, our profits were dwindling fast, while the rest of the crew was working in the part of the field with the most plentiful and biggest berries. They were so far away from us by this time we couldn't even hear their radios.

Ken and I were small dots at the edge of a vast landscape of berry bushes. It was deadly quiet. I glanced at the row beside ours, which showed many more missed berries than ours did. I felt the bushes laughing at us. It was obvious. Ken and I were being singled out unfairly. Had she heard us mocking her? Did she have it in for preachers' kids? Why did she spite us so? Maybe she was trying to get us to quit. I had an idea.

"Ken, drop everything," I said. "We're leaving."

"What do you mean?"

"She's full of crap. Let's quit."

"And go where?"

"Home. We can walk. This is your birthday, we shouldn't even be here."

"I'm not walking all the way home."

"Well, stay here then. I'm not slaving for the oppressor anymore."

It would be a long walk on blistering tar roads for two miles into town, but leaving on account of Ken's birthday was only half of my plan. What I didn't say was if we told Dad we were fired, we could quit the rest of picking season.

"We can't leave," Ken said. "Aunt Jemima will kill us."

"She'll never see us again, trust me. I'm going by myself if you don't come."

Ken didn't want to be left alone under Jemima's thumb. We finally dropped everything and walked away. At the end of our row we looked both ways and ran to the road and then down the road toward town until we couldn't be seen—free at last. We walked. It was hot, but it was better than staying. The raspberries were for the birds, just like strawberries were. We weren't making more than four or five dollars a day with her hanging on our every move. We walked for a couple of hours, stopping to explore ditches. When we finally got home, we saw Don standing in the driveway.

"Dad's waiting for you guys."

We looked past Don to the house. Dad was standing in the shadow of the breezeway.

"What are you guys doing home?" he said before we'd even reached the door.

"We told Aunt Jemima it was Ken's birthday, and we should get to take the day off, and then she fire—"

"So you just walked home?" Dad stared in disbelief.

"We're not picking for her anymore. She just keeps making us go back over our row. Besides, she fired us."

"No one fired you. Mrs. Witherspoon called. They didn't know where you'd gone and were worried about you."

We'd been caught. Dad seemed more embarrassed than anything else. He went into the house to grab the car keys and came right out.

"Get in the car," he said and sighed. "We're going back to talk with Mrs. Witherspoon."

We drove back in silence. I stared out the window at the hard miles we'd put behind us but were coming back to us in minutes. Dad was making us go back over our road, I thought. Here come da judge.

When we got back to the berry field, we met Mrs. Witherspoon and Aunt Jemima under the sweeping cherry tree by the farmhouse. Three chairs were waiting for Dad, Ken, and me. A conference had been arranged.

Mrs. Witherspoon told us how worried they were when they found we were gone and how grateful she was that nothing had happened to us. It was their responsibility, she said, to make sure their workers were safe and taken care of. I glance at Aunt Jemima. She was still wearing her sun bonnet even under the shade of the tree. Her eyes stared out like two holes in a slice of well-done toast. I leaned in and thought I saw tears in her eyes.

Mrs. Witherspoon asked us what led us to taking such a drastic step like walking all the way home.

"Uhm." I cleared my throat. "Aunt Jem— I mean . . ." After all we'd been through, I still didn't know her name. "She . . . kept making us go over our row, three times, and it was Ken's birthday."

Ken looked up wide-eyed, not wanting to take any blame for something that wasn't his idea. Mrs. Witherspoon assured us again, mostly for Dad's benefit, that they always did their best to make sure their workers were treated fairly. I wondered if she thought leaving two kids alone on the outskirts of the farm while everyone else was clear off on the other end picking the best berries was treating her workers fairly. Witherspoon, in her typically cheerful demeanor, promised to give us a fair shake.

"You're not going to fire us?" I said, losing hope.

"Oh, no, we're not going to fire you," she smiled. "We need you the rest of the way."

Aunt Jemima looked as disappointed as I was.

"The rest of the way," we learned, meant another four days, which sounded like an eternity, but Mrs. Witherspoon promised we would pick alongside everyone else. She asked if we could manage that. Ken rubbed his hands anxiously on his berry-stained pants and nodded, eager to get out of the intervention. I shrugged apathetically in agreement.

We finished out that day and celebrated Ken's birthday after work with a big water fight in the backyard. We ate Ken's favorite supper—meatloaf—topped off with homemade chocolate cake and ice cream.

We didn't see much of Aunt Jemima for the rest of the season, other than when she was sitting on a stack of flats with a cigarette dangling from her lips as she briefly muttered something to the checker. She stared at the feet of pickers passing by. Our ordeal seemed to have been a demotion of sorts for her, but I couldn't feel sorry for her. Over the last four days, we had to re-pick our row only once and made about thirty-five dollars each, our best money of the season.

At the end of our last day, Dad congratulated us on a job well done. He put down his fork at the supper table.

"So you know why you can't just walk off a job, right?" he said calmly. "Think about this—what if your next boss calls Mrs. Witherspoon and asks how you were as workers? If she says you quit without notice, do you think you're going to get hired by the next boss?"

"I don't know," I said. "Maybe not, I suppose."

"Whether you think you're in the right or not, you have to settle your disputes with your boss. These things follow you."

He spoke the last as if he knew from experience what he was talking about. I could only imagine he'd had plenty of people in his past churches who had time to get to know his faults, and plenty of them had probably passed on to the elders in the Sumas church what they knew, right or wrong. There was no way for a pastor to put his record behind him. Even if he moved to the farthest port on the edge of the continent, gossip followed like mice on a ship.

Mom said we could stay up late that night to watch *Gilligan's Island* and *Gunsmoke*, but we were too tired and went to bed right after supper.

I stared up from my bunk at the bottom of Ken's.

"Hey, Ken."

"Yeah."

I pushed up on his mattress with my foot a couple times. "Here come da judge, here come da judge."

"Cut it out."

"Were you mad at me when we took off on your birthday?"

"No, I wanted to go, too."

"Blood is thicker than berries, ain't it?"

"Yeah."

"Hey," I said, "do you want to play baseball next summer?"

"I just want to sleep."

I thought about Peggy again for the first time since the strawberry fields.

"Do you know Peggy Allen?" I asked.

But Ken was already asleep. When I closed my eyes, I saw nothing but raspberry bushes with orange and green berries. I opened my eyes and looked at my hands. I wondered how long it would take for the berry stains to wash off.

— Chapter 16 —

Closing Argument

We had four guns in the house, which we kept in the pantry by the back door—two shotguns for game birds, a 22 rifle for rabbits, and a BB gun for dicking around. They had been there since before I was born. Guns were simply a part of life, and it never crossed our minds that we shouldn't have them.

Having four guns was actually nothing compared to what some families had. One kid from across town said his dad had a whole room full, and his dad would show them to me if I came to his house, so I did. The dad chatted me up as if he hadn't had a visitor for days and finally asked if I'd like to see his guns. He led me to a back room, talking non-stop, sniffing habitually at pauses in his monologue. He opened a door to reveal a vast arsenal of shotguns, rifles, and pistols—on racks, standing in corners, and lying on tables. A number of them created a picket fence along one wall.

"All legal," he said confidently, yanking on his belt, as if I might challenge him on their legitimacy. He sniffed as he pulled out several trays that sagged with an assortment of bullets and shotgun shells. "There's amo here for every gun in this room, ready to go at a moment's notice." He didn't say what kind of "notice" he was expecting, and I didn't ask.

On one table, lying in a freshly opened box, was a shiny new double-barreled shotgun.

"Come with me," he said, picking up the shotgun and leading me out back to the garage. He opened a vice. "Okay, place your hand in there please . . . just kidding." His belly bounced as he laughed. He fit his gun into the vice and measured off a predetermined length on the barrel. Then he took a hacksaw and sawed off the barrel, leaving a foot of it intact.

"Still legal length," he said, blowing on his fresh cut and holding out his refurbished shotgun waist high in one hand. It looked like an oversized pistol. He pointed it at the door and said, "If they come for my guns, this is what they get," and pulled both triggers in quick succession—click, click. His sniffing stopped and the smile left his face.

I told him I had to go home for lunch, turned, and ran five blocks before slowing to a walk back on familiar ground. I stopped on the bridge to watch the creek. I gathered from my visit with the kid's dad that guns were good not only for hunting and protecting yourself but also for protecting your guns.

I was allowed to use only the BB gun before I was thirteen. But the BB gun lost my interest over time as it lost power. At a mere thirty yards we had to aim high to account for the arch of the BB. Then our neighbor, Fred, provided our salvation when he came over to the house to show us his new gun—a pellet air rifle. Ken and I followed Fred around town, watching him shoot at cans and posts, until he let us take a couple shots ourselves.

"Here, let me pump it up for you first," he told me, giving the gun several pumps. "See you hit that bottle over there."

I stared down the barrel at a beer bottle by Old Man Tanner's shed. The sights on the gun were so precise, the feel of it so light, that it felt harmless. I took aim and pulled the trigger but missed. I tried a second time and knocked the top off the bottle at the neck. I took a few steps back and hit it again with a satisfying shatter. Excitement rose in my chest. The pellet gun was a new kind of power.

Ken and I had never asked Dad for a pellet gun of our own. They were too expensive, and we'd have to give him a good reason to have one. He'd just look at us wide-eyed as if we'd asked him for a new Jaguar and say what for? The thing about Dad was, if we couldn't argue our case, our chances of getting what we wanted were slim to none. The argument that everybody else had one wasn't a good reason. That Don and Dale had shotguns, and a 22, didn't go over either on account of our brothers being several years older. And, "we need a pellet gun for practice" just begged the question down the same path of "What for? Practice for killing things?"

The assertion was difficult to deny. Killing was a gun's ultimate aim, a simple truth we had learned from multiple episodes of *Gunsmoke*—when you see a cowboy shooting at cans in the desert, it's always a warm-up for the real thing. There stood Marshall Dillon by show's end, gun drawn, looking down at the bad guy's corpse in the dust of Main Street in downtown Dodge. Dillon's smoking gun was the closing argument of every scenario.

We learned the same lesson when Don walked in the back door after a hunt with his closing argument in hand and a fistful of pheasants raised shoulder high, the pheasants' star-studded breasts puffed out as far as the hunter's. Pheasant was good eating, and what we didn't eat we gave away. But as much as Mom and Dad loved a good pheasant dinner, I knew having guns in the house was an uneasy alliance for them.

Fred, Ken, and I passed Fred's new pellet gun back and forth just to feel the smooth wood stock, the clean, steel grey barrel, the balance of it, and the rush of believing ourselves to be older than we were. One dream of my future self was as Davy Crockett, living off the land in a cabin in the mountains along a stream, where I would own nothing and owe nothing to anyone. I would have a gun and a knife and hunt whatever I needed for food, doing what I was made to do as I commanded the woods with the confidence of a grizzly. I put my nose to the barrel of Fred's gun and breathed in the metallic aroma. I was getting itchy to shoot real game.

A lazy afternoon mist was clearing over the tops of the Lombardi poplars near the church. Fred put a pellet in the chamber and pumped his gun more times than usual. He would need power, lots of it, for the shot in front him. He was looking up to the top of one of the poplars where a flock of starlings roosted. The shot was nearly impossible, the poplar standing as high as a silo, far above the church steeple, the starlings only vague black dots against the gray sky. Their squeals and chimes dribbled like the rain trickling down the church's drain spout. Ken and I suggested he shouldn't waste a pellet, but as if he hadn't even heard us, Fred rested his gun against the corner of the church and took aim.

There was a puff of air from the gun, a split second's delay, and one starling dislodged itself, flapping helplessly toward the ground in a long, slow spiral, bouncing off branches, until it finally landed in the leaves at the base of the tree. Without a word, Fred went to retrieve the dead starling as if this were simply routine.

Fred's masterful shots left us incredulous and inspired. Once, he took down a pigeon in full flight with our failing BB gun. Another time, a kid challenged Fred to shoot him with the BB gun as he stood halfway across the school playground because he didn't think Fred could hit him at such long range. The shot would require a significant arch to correct for distance. The kid was so confident he didn't even cover his face. Fred pulled the trigger, and a couple of seconds later the kid was lifting his shirt and rubbing his stomach where the BB had left a red welt just above his navel.

One morning, after Fred had promised us a chance to shoot at real game, we were walking up Johnson Creek scanning the trees and stopped at a patch of blackberries. A number of birds flitted up and down on the arched stems. One settled on a top branch in the briars, moving its head back and forth and twitching its wings nervously. Fred said it was my shot and gave me his gun. I lifted it to my shoulder and took aim. It was my first shot at a living thing. I was shaking.

The bird in my sights looked impossibly small compared to the beer bottles and cans I'd been practicing on. I could hear my older brother Don in the back of my mind—"Breathe in and hold it. Fill the notch with the bead at the end of the barrel." The bead wavered in and out of the notch. My target moved and settled again. "Now squeeze the trigger, don't jerk it . . . and don't be a jerk," he added in my mind with a touch of humor. That eased my nerves and steadied the gun.

The gun gave my shoulder a firm nudge as the puff of air forced out the pellet. The bird tipped from its perch and fell.

"You got it!" Fred shouted.

I froze with the gun still at my shoulder. Fred emerged from the blackberries, briars grabbing at his sweatshirt, and dropped a house sparrow into my hand. It was warm in my palm, soft as cotton, exquisite in color and detail—brown wings, gray cap, and a patch of black just under the chin, like a baby's bib. Its small dark eye stared up at me. I didn't feel the way I expected to feel. I expected I'd feel excited and proud. But I just stared as a strange sensation of guilt and awe tumbled inside me. Somehow I knew I'd passed through a door that I could never retreat back through again.

The rest of the day my head was swimming with the images of our hunt. I carried my kill, wrapped in Kleenex, to our graveyard behind the garage at the edge of the garden. It was an area we designated for animals that had met their ends in one way or another. Other birds lay there, having slammed themselves headlong into our picture window thinking they'd just sighted a grove in the window's reflection. Pets dead from age or from meeting with cars rested there. Our dog Skip was recently buried there. Don found her dead on the highway that year after she'd taken off on a hunt of her own. Fred's cat lay there too after a husky caught her in its jaws. His cat had lain paralyzed after the attack, still breathing, until a man passing by stepped on her neck to cut off her air and finish her suffering, out of mercy, he said.

But the sparrow was not an accident, and my conscience was paying a price. That night I lay awake in my bunk, staring up at the slats suspending Ken above me like a bird on a limb. The day flickered like a slide show through my mind—the raised pellet gun, the sparrow tumbling through blackberry brambles, and Fred's dispassionate gaze. In my sleep the sparrow's beak gaped as if to speak. I strained to hear but no words formed. As its one eye peered up at me, the other bore a hole into my palm clear through my hand. I sat up in bed, sweating, and rubbed my hand. I called for Ken, and then Keith, but neither responded.

My parents believed man was endowed with a spirit and intellect animals did not possess. According to our Dutch reformed doctrine, man was "the crown of creation," and animals were under man's dominion. Some said animals would not go to heaven, so it was best not to love them too much. But my doubts about this idea, along with doubts about shooting the sparrow, prodded at my chest like a woodpecker on a young tree. I had questions.

"Dad, where do animals go when they die if they don't go to heaven?" I asked, poking at my breakfast cereal with a spoon.

Dad gazed up from his fried egg. Here were more animal questions from one of his boys. He wondered where it was going this time.

"When we eat roast beef, we kill cows, right?" I continued. "So where do they go after they die?"

"We kill cows because we need to eat, like your snake Bomber needed to eat those frogs, right?" Dad said.

"And we can kill animals if they're pests, too, right? Don said we can kill all the starlings and house sparrows we want because they're invaders from England, and they crowd out native species. They're nest robbers, so it's okay to kill them, right? But then if we kill them, do they go to heaven?"

There was a long pause. Dad seldom stated his beliefs without careful thought. He understood his role as a pastor never more so than when it came to influencing young minds. Keith, six years old, listened, spooning cereal over the lip of his bowl into his mouth.

"I don't like the thinking that says you can kill things just because they aren't native to our country," Dad said finally. "Your grandparents immigrated from Holland. Do you think it would have been right for people to shoot at them? Or, how about the people coming here from Asia?"

"Well, I'll shoot them *before* they get here if I go to Vietnam," I blurted.

"You're not going to Vietnam," he said solemnly. It sounded more like a prayer than a statement. "And war is not hunting. You're not just shooting in war, you're being shot at."

"But I'll be a moving target."

Ken asked, "What are you going to do, fly away like a bird?"

"Yeah, if I'm flying a jet, I will." I flew my spoon over my cereal and dropped an imaginary bomb, and on its next turn my spoon took a nose dive into the bowl.

The conversation had meandered, and Dad didn't know what more to say. He sometimes saw silence as the best answer. He was also likely considering the possibility Don and Dale may be off to the war if it didn't end soon.

"Everybody's killing stuff all the time," I said, thoughts of death still playing in my head. "Mom killed two baby chicks for breakfast when she fried your eggs."

Dad looked down at his plate, shook his head at his son's persistence, and laughed. He'd had more than a few debates with his kids, but this was one of the more bizarre ones.

Mom interjected, back-lit angelically in a halo of light from the open fridge. "Did somebody say I killed something? I did no such thing."

Dad tried to wrap it up and put the discussion to bed with his closing argument. "Every living creature God gave us for food—vegetable or animal. But that's the only killing that's allowed—for eating. And no, animals and plants do not go to heaven. As far as we know."

So not only had I killed something that I had not meant for food, but the sparrow also would not find its way to heaven. Confusion and guilt settled in my stomach. Dad picked up a whole egg yolk from his plate with his fork and deftly flipped it to the back of his mouth with a shout, "There!"

"Now Pete, come on," she said. "Don't teach them to do that."

Keith piped up, "Mom, can I have an egg too?"

Dad tipped his head back and howled, the gold caps on his teeth gleaming amid egg yolk, while Mom cracked another egg in the frying pan.

— Chapter 17 —

Splendor

The "animal conversation" with Dad convinced me to quit hunting birds, for awhile anyway. I continued shooting at junk, but the thrill of firing a gun was gone. Not even my classmates' stories about their shooting exploits got me to take it seriously anymore. But a few years later, when I turned thirteen, Don said I was old enough to come duck hunting with him. Dad would approve, he said, as we could eat the ducks we shot. He noticed my hesitation.

"Think of it like this—it's introduced predation," Don said. "We're culling the flocks like any other predator would do. The hunters get to eat, but it's good for the ducks too. Otherwise they overpopulate and starve." He said it with a straightforward conviction that always made things seem simpler than they were.

I suggested I'd just follow along the first time, and if he shot anything, I'd let him eat it. But he said the only real way to get into hunting was with a bang.

"Here," he said, "take a couple practice shots just to get the feel of it. You don't exactly aim with a shotgun, you point."

He handed me the 20-gage shotgun we kept stored in our pantry. It felt heavy and awkward. He set a can on a fence post. I raised the barrel and pointed. The sound was deafening, and the gun bucked my shoulder with a force I would not forget. The can on the post disappeared. The acrid smell of gunpowder rose to my nose as I ejected the spent shell from the gun chamber with a metallic clack-clack. The exhilaration of shooting, which I'd first felt shooting Fred's pellet gun, returned instantly and with greater intensity.

We headed for the fields along Johnson Creek just outside of town. Hunting ducks was in a league where shooting a pellet gun was child's play.

We plodded through soggy fields of corn stubble for a tedious, unproductive two hours, squeezing through barbwire fences and covering our heads against the intermittent rain. Neither of us had anything to show for our hunt but mud-laden boots and tired arms from lugging shotguns. We hadn't seen a single duck within range or taken a single shot. The rain drizzled into every pore down to the bone, and I was sick of it.

Following Don's steps, I mumbled a disgruntled chant to myself. "Lotsa muck and no luck with fuckin' ducks." I asked Don, "Hey, all this walking, when are we going to shoot at something?"

"That's the way it goes," he said. "Sometimes you get skunked. Just keep your finger off that trigger and keep the safety on unless you're sure you've got a decent shot."

We paused, finally on the way back to the car, as Don scanned the sky.

"They're kinda skittish today," he said, trying to make excuses for our bad luck. "There's been so many hunters through here already, the ducks have probably learned to keep their distance. They probably know when the last day of hunting season is and only show up after that."

"Come on, really?"

"That's what they say."

"The ducks say that?"

Don laughed. "The hunters, knucklehead."

"Smart ducks."

"Yep, smarter than us evidently."

Crawling through the last fence on our route, Don got stuck halfway when the barbed wire snagged on his jacket.

"Dadgumit. Here," he said, handing me his 12-gauge pump action. I was amazed at how much bigger it was than my 20-gauge. "Well don't just stand there, help me out."

I leaned the guns against the fence and unhooked him from the barbwire to let him pass through. The muck was getting to him too, and I was glad he was ready to quit. But I liked being there with him. The weather was miserable, and we had got skunked, but my older brother was teaching me how to hunt like Davy Crockett in order to eat, not how to shoot sparrows like Tom Sawyer just for fun. I thought, how many kids got that?

"We'll try again another day," Don said.

"Sure."

If we'd stopped and thought about it, we'd have recognized a sad irony. While we were negotiating mud-soaked fields, itching to get a shot at a duck, Dale, who had enlisted in the army, would probably soon be halfway across the world in Vietnam. He'd be negotiating muck and barbwire himself, getting shot at, and trying not to be the unlucky duck to be culled for the greater good of the flock. Supposedly, I'd get my chance too if the war kept on, but I was thirteen, and the war seemed so far away.

Before we reached the car, Don and I stopped to look one more time through an opening in the trees by the creek. Then, just as we turned to walk on, the creek exploded with a flurry of slapping on the water followed by a distinct whistling sound as wings churned through the air. The blood rush through me so fast I felt like I could fly myself. Our guns automatically went to our shoulders as if of their own accord.

"Never mind," Don said, lowering his gun, "they're heading down the creek." We saw flashes of them through the bare branches along the creek. They were keeping low. Then two of the ducks flared left like fighter jets executing a ditch maneuver, crossing in front of us about a hundred yards off over the open field.

"Ah shoot! Way out of range," Don said.

But I was tracking them with my gun, giving a good ten-foot lead and a slight arc for distance. I pulled the trigger. Kablam!

"Jeepers!" Don jumped at the blast of my gun right beside him.

One of the ducks descended, flapping helplessly, trying to stay airborne. We both stood stunned and amazed.

"What? You hit one. I cannot believe that," Don said. He rubbed at his ear to stop it ringing. "I meant 'oh shoot' as in 'don't shoot.' Not 'shoot' as in 'shoot.'"

"I know what you meant but I already made up my mind. We've been out here a whole two hours without a dadgum thing, and I wanted to shoot!"

Don just stared in disbelief. Even given the longer range of his 12-gauge, he had taken a pass on the shot. It dawned on me then that I hadn't needed Don's say-so. It would be my decision from now on when and what to shoot.

My heart raced as we approached the fallen duck. It was a mallard hen. I had only wounded it. It flopped a couple of times trying to get away. Don grabbed it by its head and twirled it like a lasso at our feet until we heard its neck snap.

"There you go," he said. He held the duck out to me with a look of admiration for his hunting prodigy. "Good shot, man, that's dinner."

I took the hen by the head, letting it swing nonchalantly at my side like a baseball mitt after a ballgame. We walked side by side to the car, Don repeating, "I can't believe it . . . with a 20-gauge." He laughed.

At home I set the mallard down on the garage floor on some newsprint with a picture of an aircraft carrier off the shores of Vietnam. Don explained again how I should clean the duck.

"Were you watching last time I did this? You hang it up and then cut it right here at the neck." He indicated the spot with his small finger. "Then just peel the skin back all the way down to its tail, help it along with the knife if you have to, and after that just open up the rear end and pull out the guts."

I stared blankly at the limp bird and swallowed. Left to myself, I hung the duck with a piece of twine tied around its neck and took a deep breath. The duck's purple iridescent wing bars flashed as she twirled in the noose, a pirouette at the finale of a performance of a lifetime, her transcendent splendor displayed to the world.

I went into the house and told Don he should clean the duck because I'd just botch the job, but he would hear none of it. I'd shot it, he said, it was my kill, and I had to clean it. At first, I thought he was saying this out of spite because I'd taken the shot he'd passed on, but he was right. I had to finish what I'd ended. What I didn't tell him was that I just didn't have the strength to do it. I couldn't cut into that beautiful bird, which had by any measure lived its life with dignity and grace. I wondered what her mate was doing just then. Had he come flying back to look for her? I couldn't butcher her, much less eat her, but she wasn't coming back to life either. After deliberating for a minute, I knew the only thing I could do. I cut the duck free from the noose and brought it to the garbage can, where I quietly disposed of it.

It didn't take Dad long to discover the duck. After bringing out the garbage the next day, he came to me and Don.

"Who put that duck in the garbage can?"

Don didn't say anything, and I looked down.

"Why didn't you clean it?"

I couldn't answer, confounded with a mix of failure and guilt. I was no Davy Crockett. The word "anger" would not rightly describe what I saw in my dad's face just then. What I saw was anguish, grief, and disbelief all at once. After collecting himself, he spoke to me, tears in his eyes.

"Haven't you learned?" He took a deep breath, exasperated, and said, "You never take an animal's life . . . one of God's creatures . . . just for sport, and just leave it. Never." He turned away, saying something under his breath that sounded like a lament between him and God.

The sickness I felt after that lasted days, when I couldn't face my dad. I didn't have a valid explanation. I only knew that day was the end of guns for me.

Months later, Don came home one day with binoculars hanging from his neck. He had been bird watching, or birding, as it was affectionately known among bird watching advocates. It had apparently ushered in a whole new world for him. He had retired the shotguns and shells to the back shelf and bought the binoculars and a bird identification book. His conversion was nothing short of miraculous. He had noticeably changed, turned soft.

"So, how do you bird watch?" I wanted to know.

"Come with me and watch. If you see a bird you like, you point your binoculars at it till you get it in your sights."

"And take your shot?" I joked.

Don didn't laugh. "Nope, no more shooting."

Don, Ken, and I drove to the woods west of Sumas and took a trail Don knew. We walked it, making as little noise as possible.

"We're looking for palliated woodpeckers," Don said. "A guy said he saw one in this area. But if you see anything at all interesting, we'll all stop and look."

A couple minutes later, he was pointing to something on the ground partially hidden in the bushes. To the naked eye it seemed to be just another sparrow, but my binoculars filled my view with its brilliant colors and details. It was larger than a sparrow, with a black cape over its entire head, white-speckled wings, reddish brown sides, and a white belly. It threw its head back and let out a long high trill.

"What is that?" I asked.

"Shh. Check the book. He's in there. You have to get used to finding out for yourself."

Ken and I fumbled through our guidebook, not knowing where to start among the hundreds of images of birds. Don took the book from my hands, flipped a few pages, and pointed to a figure that resembled what we were looking at.

"Rufous-sided towhee?" I queried, reading the name and laughing. The bird flew off as if offended at hearing its name mocked.

"I said, quiet, right?" Don said.

The whole bird watching thing felt like a church service—the reverence, the attention to the preacher, which in this case were the birds at their various pulpits, and even a definitive text that told if you were right or wrong. At the back of the bird book, Don showed us a checklist where we could mark which birds we'd seen. We moved on silently, alert to movement in the trees. With practice we improved, becoming more adept at identify the birds, sometimes simply by their songs. We were like Adam and Eve naming the animals, and with each naming the hunter in me surrendered to a growing respect for the life of birds.

That winter we were driving down a single lane road to a marsh Don's friend had showed him. We pulled off and parked. Before even opening the car door, I could hear a tremendous cacophony of musical honking sounds.

"What is that?" I asked.

"Come on, you'll see." Don motioned for me to follow.

The honking became louder as we came to the edge of a small cliff that dropped off onto a forty-acre marsh, filled from one end to the other with a flock of large white birds with long necks and black bills—trumpeter swans—spread like a shag carpet half a mile wide. Swans were descending to the group with wide spread wings as others flew off. Others raised their heads, sounding out their pure, piercing trumpet calls. The chorus of thousands was deafening, unlike anything I'd ever heard in nature. No one could take this in through binoculars. I did not even raise them to my eyes. The story of the flock was not about their exquisite details in this case but in their grand call to one common and mysterious purpose. As their song washed over me, I ached with uncontainable beauty even as I ached with regret over ever killing any living thing.

At times, my brothers and I grew competitive about who could be the first to find a bird and call out its name. Disputes arose about what we'd actually seen.

"A dowitcher!"

"It can't be. The book says it only comes here in the winter."

"Well, the bird didn't read the book, did he? Anyway, if he did, he's not a literalist."

That became our standard argument in the face of ambiguity—"The bird didn't read the book"—and ended all debates. Anomalies eventually became my favorite part of our outings—the mystery—simply letting a creature be what it was without checking it off my list. Birds shouldn't be objects we "bagged," I thought, as if we were hunting them.

One day I was driving with Don near Sumas Mountain, clouds closing and parting over the foothills on a windswept day, when Don abruptly pulled the car off to the side of the road. He pointed to the top of a lone tree that looked out over a pasture.

"Kestrel," he said.

The bird was a little bigger than a robin, perched straight and tall. It rotated its head to look at us. I opened my guidebook. Another name for kestrel, it said, was "sparrow hawk." The book also had a small note—they were sometimes used by falconers to catch invasive species like sparrows and starlings. I laughed to myself. We should have been using sparrow hawks instead of guns.

The kestrel didn't budge from its sentry pose, holding its sharp, curved bill proudly, ready to hunt and rip its prey. Two dark streaks fell from its eyes down its cheeks like permanent tears, as though it carried a deep sorrow for the small creatures it had killed over its lifetime. The kestrel watched us watching him until it suddenly took flight, speeding out over the pasture on a draught of wind, the deft hunter, doing what it was made to do.

— Chapter 18 —

Gargoyles

Mr. Navis was on the phone with Dad asking if he knew where Shirley had been that afternoon. Dad gave a couple of "uhms." His kids were free-range, which involved a certain amount of letting go on my parents' part as a simple matter of keeping sanity, so he couldn't really be faulted for not knowing where all his chickens were at any given moment.

Dad braced himself. "I don't know," he said. "But I have a feeling you're going to tell me."

Mr. Navis explained that his house had been broken into and vandalized while they were gone. Clothes were taken out of the closet and scattered. All his wife's things—jewelry, perfumes, clothes—had been tossed out the window over the lawn. Shirley had been at their house when they went out, and they'd told her it was time to go home. Mr. Navis didn't know anyone else who would do anything like that.

"Thank you for letting us know," Dad said, realizing Navis's instincts were probably accurate. "We'll talk to her, and we'll pay for whatever loss you've incurred."

Shirley's voice was somber. "Yes, I did it," she said in a daze when confronted. One thing about Shirley was she'd own up to whatever she did. Her voice registered matter of fact resignation to forces beyond her control. She plucked at her eyebrows mesmerized, waiting for Dad himself to offer an explanation for what she'd just done. Nothing in Dad's pastoral training had prepared him for Shirley. He squinted in agony, surveying her face for a way through the cloud of unknowing.

The official term used to describe Shirley was "retarded." The experts, after a few years' enlightenment, adjusted the language to "mentally handicapped," later to "mentally disabled," and finally they were just using "disabled." People understandably stumbled trying to use the right word with the constantly changing terminology. Shirley nevertheless heard the term "retarded" often. Ironically, the label came most often from her disabled peers, who called each other retarded, at times to tease or antagonize and often simply as a factual descriptor rather than with any intended malice.

Shirley would ask, "Mom, am I retarded?" and Mom insisted, "No, you're our special girl," with a smile that was burdened with years of heartache over the discrimination and disadvantages Shirley felt. There was no getting around it with Shirley. She knew she was not simply special. She didn't function like others, and there was no use trying to color it in pastels. In her mind "special" begged the question, special how?

"You mean like repeating myself over and over again?" she asked. "Or playing with my Kleenex tissue all the time, and talking to strangers?"

Mom would only respond with a kiss on her forehead. "You're our special girl."

Her habit of talking to strangers was a big issue whenever we went out with her. In public places she considered herself the host of the party, greeting everyone in the store and introducing herself. People would wonder what she was trying to sell, but Shirley simply wanted to be their friend. "Can we be friends?" "Do you like me?" We'd reach our breaking point before getting out of the store.

When we told family stories around the supper table, Shirley would always elbow her way in to retell her own dramatic events. Even better, she liked hearing them retold by others. She wanted to hear it all—the good, the bad, and the embarrassing moments of her life—equally proud of her entire repertoire of life stories. In her mind, they were all acceptable for supper time sharing.

"Mom, tell the one about how I walked into the field in the snow and got lost."

We knew Shirley's top escapades by heart, but it would take a while for the sting of her indiscretions at Navis's house to wear off before that story too was added to the list for table talk.

Our family had to bear some responsibility for Shirley's rebellious behavior because of our own examples. We were a non-conformist lot. Whatever gene mutation Shirley may have had, a mutinous gene had invaded the whole Petersen gene pool. Sharon, the oldest, left home at eighteen and married a conspiracy theorist, and then raised six of her own little renegades. Don once nearly burned down an entire hectare of crops lighting a dead chicken on fire in the middle of a wheat field to see what chicken flambé looked like. The fire department caught it before it could sweep the prairies. Dale led his whole class in an act of insurrection against the high school principal at their graduation exercises with a bizarre and publicly embarrassing walk-off as their final argument, and then he signed up for the army in the middle of the Vietnam War. Nancy flew off overseas for twenty-five plus years to the leech and mosquito infested jungles of Papua New Guinea with her husband, who was in the practice of perching himself in a tree before sunrise to pray, while they raised three boys who loved making bombs and running barefoot through the jungle. Ken, a biology prof, took a teaching post at a conservative religious college in the corn belt, where he cultivated insurgent hybrid notions of Christian care of the environment, which smelled like quack weed to his superiors. Keith took off to Asia and eventually married across racial lines, a radical departure from our closed, mono-cultural milieu. And I was the family's dissident to Canada, where I spent time in lonely cafes writing poetry about the rain.

But for the grace of God, I suppose any one of us could have ended up either institutionalized or incarcerated. We weren't "normal." If Shirley required inspiration for her renegade behavior, she needed look no further than her own family.

She managed to tap into my tendency for off the wall behavior by coaxing me to do animal sounds. My repertoire grew to comprise a complete farm. The more I did the animal sounds, the more polished they became and the more I put her in stitches. And the more she enjoyed them, the more she practiced the sounds herself until she was a virtuoso in her own right. We developed our dog barks into dramatic dog fights. Her pig squeal carried a very high level of difficulty and became a tour de force. She performed it everywhere—at restaurants, church, ball games, or the grocery store. If no one was looking, the two of us might duck behind a stack of Campbell's soup for a pig squeal duet. People would look down the aisles, bewildered, trying to figure out how pigs got into the store.

"The ham's in aisle three!" someone laughed when they found us.

Like most people, Shirley had her obsessions and various cravings. First it was The Monkees pop group. She begged until she had all the Monkees vinyls and paraphernalia. She did the monkey dance to every song, even to non-Monkees songs. Next she latched on to the Beatles, which was a big relief. If we had to listen non-stop, we at least deserved good music.

There were also phrases and questions she couldn't let go of. We heard incessantly, "Do you love me?" and "Can you give me a hug?" and "Am I your sister?" betraying her deep insecurity about her place in the family.

Starting back when she was six, Mom and Dad enrolled Shirley in special boarding schools for the mentally handicapped. In the 50's and 60's institutions were the popular means of caring for the disabled, even disabled kids. They had specialists, trained professionals, who supposedly knew more than we did. It was agonizing for Mom to let her go, but Mom accepted her own lack of know-how and objectivity, and Dad had his limitations, as well, with patience. And after all, they had seven other kids, three younger than Shirley, who were not any easier to deal with. Wisdom dictated putting her "in better hands," while we would pick her up and bring her home for holidays and on some weekends.

As young kids, Shirley and I were good pals, and I think I silently grieved her exile because thinking of her made me sad. Perhaps none of us could give words to our feelings about her absence. In the end, we simply adapted to the ebb and flow of Shirley's comings and goings.

Shirley herself seemed to be as happy to come home as to go to back again so she could be with her friends, but being away must have nevertheless taken a toll she could only express through her obsessive questions. "Do you love me?" was one that persisted over all others.

And the answer was always the same. "Of course, you know that we love you, you don't need to ask." This we often followed with a sigh of exasperation for the multiple times we had to answer the same question.

No matter how many times we hugged her and affirmed our devotion to her, it was not enough. I broke at the end of my rope numerous times. "Stop asking me!" And she would stomp off complaining that I didn't love her anymore, and then I'd feel guilty.

"We all lose our patience sometimes," Mom told me. "But you're good with her."

"Think so?"

"Have you ever thought of working with special ed kids?"

"You mean, 'when I grow up'?" I said, not feeling I could ever grow up enough to qualify for such a task.

Years later, after I'd supposedly grown up, I was visiting Shirley, Mom, and Dad during Christmas break while they were living in Michigan. They had settled into a live-in arrangement for Shirley as she went out daily to a combination of factory work and school.

Shirley was still a big Beatles fan, I learned. I had to give her credit for loyalty after all those years. She was still nursing an assortment of cravings. Now she was all about tiaras.

"Why do you want a tiara?" I asked.

"I want to be a princess!" She put on her best princess smile, revealing two rows of poorly attended teeth.

My instinct was to discourage her from vices of vanity and self-recognition, but trying to tell Shirley to forget about the tiara was like blowing seeds off a dandelion head that would take root elsewhere. My words simply fanned her pleas with greater intensity.

Mom put a hand on my shoulder and whispered for me to take her out and look around.

"Just get her one. A tiara's not going to hurt anyone."

I drove Shirley to Kmart through falling snow. It was feeling like Christmas. In the toy section we found some plastic tiaras packaged in cellophane. For Shirley, this was the discovery of jewels at the bottom of a treasure chest. I told her if she stopped bugging me, I'd buy one for her. That started her in singing, "She loves you, yea, yea, yea," along with the Monkees dance right there in the store. She followed that with a loud, "Yee haw!" Her voice echoed down the aisles.

"Can I wear it now?" she asked as she proceeded to rip the tiara from its package and put it on her head. The glass jewels in the plastic frame sparkled under the fluorescent lights. I adjusted the tiara so that at least it was on straight.

"Karl, am I your princess?"

"No, you're my big sister," I said. "Don't yell so loud." The old feelings of exasperation came flooding back.

"Okay, Karl," she apologized. "I'll yell softly, okay?"

"Okay," I sighed.

"Do you love me, Karl?"

"You know I love you. Now stop asking."

At the checkout, she turned and smiled to make sure everyone in line saw her in her new tiara. She smiled at the clerk. "How do I look?"

"Just great, honey," the clerk smiled back.

On the way to the car, Shirley tapped me on the arm. "Karl, did you hear that? She called me honey. Do I look good?"

"Fantastic," I said impatiently. "Hop in."

As I backed the car out of our parking spot, Shirley noticed a man in a full beard walking by and rolled down the window so he could get the full view of her tiara. She waved as if she were in a motorcade on her way to Buckingham Palace.

"Are you Santa Claus?" she asked, recognizing their mutual royalty. "I'm a princess."

The man laughed, his feet shuffling over the snow-packed pavement.

"Do you love me?" Shirley asked.

He wrinkled his brow and slipped briefly. "Do I know you?"

I pulled Shirley's hand back inside the window. "Don't ask strange guys if they love you."

She bawled and scolded me all the way home as I fishtailed through snow down a poorly lit back street. I wished intensely for her to grow up and leave her obsessive yearnings.

Feeling glum about my attitude, she didn't wear her tiara for a couple of days, and I was hopeful she'd gotten the princess thing out of her system now that she owned a tiara. But she soon returned to her original conviction that she was royalty. She wore the tiara everywhere, not only at home but also to lunch at Denny's, to the grocery store, and on our periodic walks, continuing to announce to her unsuspecting subjects that she was the princess they never knew they had.

After some reflecting, I finally told her that, yes, she was a princess because she was special to me and her family, as well as to God. I told her she could rule the kingdom if she would only put on a bit of humility and keep the fact of her royalty to herself. And I told her she also had to stop singing "I am the Walrus" because it wasn't becoming of a princess.

"Thank you, brother Karl!"

The acknowledgement was all that mattered. We had struck a deal. She had won me over, and she in turn was pleasantly quiet, for a time. I kicked myself for not having come to this point sooner.

Not far from the house, on the shore of Lake Michigan, was a beautiful state park where Shirley loved taking outings with her siblings. One bright, cold morning, she said she wanted to go for a walk through the fresh snow. I told her to bundle up and went to look for my mitts. When I returned, she was already waiting by the door in her fiberfill winter coat, ballooned out like a blimp, the hood nearly swallowing her head. The Michelin Man came to mind.

"Come on, Karl, it's getting hot in here," she said, glancing down at her blimp. "Let's go."

Shirley was blessed with an unassuming wit that often hit people broadside. She could crack up the most hardened cynic. She couldn't see why I was laughing, but seeing me happy put her in a good mood.

"Yee, hee, hee! Shall I bring my tiara?" She held it up, her smile beaming out through the hole in her hood.

"And wear it under your hood? That wouldn't be very comfortable."

"No, over my hood, silly, like this." She put on the tiara, an image I would not easily erase from my mind—Michelin Man in a tiara.

"Sure," I said, unable to contain my laughter. "Looks good."

At the park, we followed a path packed down by other ambitious walkers. Shirley was delighted just to be doing something special with her brother. The displeasure I'd shown about the whole tiara saga had invoked a sadness in me that echoed back in time to memories of past struggles and indecipherable feelings over how best to deal with Shirley. I had come to see her and my parents for Christmas and had acted like an ogre, unable to show patience with her, and it exposed something in me I hated.

Our trail wove through broadleaf woods stripped after the leaf fall to spindles that clashed and clattered like bare bones in gusts of wind from the lake. The quiet was deafening, penetrated only by the snow crunching under our feet. Occasionally, in a gust, the trees shook loose large shawls of snow down over us.

Out of the stillness, I heard a loud bird call. I turned to see Shirley, looking up into the trees with her hands cupped to her mouth, imitating a near flawless crow call. A crow sat gawking down at her.

"Where did you learn the crow call," I asked.

"From the crows, dummy! Karl, do you love crows?"

"Love them? Uhm."

It wasn't the phrase I would have chosen. Crows woke people up, raided the nests of song birds, and were capable of destroying the peace of a northern wood with raucous chatter. I had shot a few in my past before I'd become a birdwatcher.

Then the thought struck me—the crow was her soul mate. She had found a creature like her, one that lived on the margins, misunderstood by many, yet one that understood her boisterous nature and cries for acceptance. Crows, like her, were subject to ridicule. And crows understood the inclination to raid someone's home and inexplicably pick up shiny objects like jewelry and tiaras.

Shirley called to the crow again. The crow called back. She continued in undistracted conversation. I envied her free spirit and innocence.

"Nice," I said. "It likes you."

As we walked on, she asked, "Karl, am I retarded?"

"No," I said. "I am."

"Yes, you are, Karl!" she said triumphantly, "You *are* retarded!" as though heaven had opened and the wisdom she'd been trying to impart for so long had finally descended on me. "You and me, honey!"

It was a simple truth—I was as retarded as she was. The acknowledgement filled me with a lightness I hadn't felt for a long time.

"What about Don?" she asked. "Is he retarded?"

"Yep, Don too."

"The three stooges, right Karl? You and me and Don. Yee! Haw!" Then she proceeded to name her other siblings, asking whether they were retarded also.

"How about Ken?"

"Yes, even Ken. He's been a vandal in his time too, you know, so don't feel bad."

"And Keith? Is he retarded?"

"Yes, everybody is." Then I said, more to myself than to her, "You look at anyone long enough, you'll find something missing, like a part of them never grew up."

At the end of the trail, we stood at the top of a sand dune overlooking Lake Michigan. Up and down the beach there stood a startling display. Hundreds of ice sculptures hewn by the wind and surf rose from the shore. They had been shaped by successive waves freezing in new layers over old, creating a vast, collective masterpiece. The sculptures stood at the lake's edge with a grotesque grandeur, like a pantheon of human-sized gargoyles, contorting nightmarishly one upon the other in a tumult of shared agony. Some were hunched, others reached skyward, open-mouthed, and each shone brilliantly in the low, frigid light with an otherworldly luster. Their crests glittered with a blue translucence like tiaras on a crowd of mutant princesses.

Laughter welled up in me, struggling through tears, blue light breaking through pain. Shirley looked at me.

"Karl, I think you need a hug." She reached out and pulled me into her Michelin Man coat, which exhaled with a sigh.

"You and me, right?" she said softly.

Our hug knocked her tiara sideways, and one of its glass jewels poked me in the cheek.

"Do you love me?" I asked her.

"Yes I do, you know that I love you. Ask me again, Karl."

Chapter 19

Crimes

My break-and-entry phase started fairly innocently though the school board didn't see it that way. I was really hooked on basketball at the time and wanted to become a sharpshooter for our junior high school team. My dribbling was improving, and I was developing a decent jump shot, but my small size worked against me. I needed some kind of extra advantage. Coaches told me the only answer was practice and another year's growth. I wasn't waiting a year, that was for sure, but the town had no public courts to practice on. The only half-decent basketball hoop was at Arthur's house, and things there were still a bit raw after he popped our Wilson basketball on a nail.

I discovered a potential solution. It seemed a shame to me that the school gym was locked up on weekends, only two blocks from our house. This was enough to justify my scheme.

I had discovered an easy way through security at the gym. The only two windows were in the two locker rooms. The windows were kept locked by a simple L-shaped latch. When rotated a quarter turn, the latch would lock or unlock the window. My plan would require complete secrecy and would have to be an inside job.

The genius of the plan was that only two people need be involved, and I had a ready-made accomplice—my brother Ken—who had break-and-entry experience at the Assumptions Church. He would never squeal. Because of his record, he knew I could easily expose him if blackmail became necessary. Even so, total secrecy was a slight challenge because word always spread in our school as quickly and invisibly as a flu virus. Finding a person on the inside, on the other hand, was straightforward. The obvious choice to pull it off was me because *I* was on the inside.

On Friday, during the last recess, I went casually into the boys' locker room, which didn't actually have lockers. There was simply a bench against the wall and the window above the bench about six feet off the floor. I stepped onto the bench and made sure no one was coming into the room behind me. I reached up and turned the L-latch to unlock the window, leaving the window itself closed. Now it could be opened easily from the outside by pulling it out and up to a forty-five degree angle.

The small detail of the turned latch would hardly be noticed unless the janitor happened to look up on his way through the change room. The window was small but large enough for me to squeeze through. I'd learned how to use my size to great advantage on many occasions in sports, in fights, and in tight spots like this. And I would have Ken as backup. The plan was so flawless it wasn't funny.

Ken knew nothing of my plan until Saturday morning. I coaxed him outside on the presumption that I had to show him something I found down by the creek.

"In the rain?" he said.

"We won't rust."

We crossed the bridge and stopped at the school grounds. I stood under the gym window. Ken looked at me, puzzled.

"What are you doing?"

"Put your hands together and give me a boost. I just wanna take a peek through the window, I think I heard something inside. It might be a burglar."

I stepped up on Ken's hands and pried the window open with my finger tips. Before Ken could ask what I was up to, I pulled myself over the window ledge, hung there for a moment, jackknifed half in and half out, and then slipped through to the inside.

"Ken, go around to the door! I'll open it!" My voice echoed off the cinderblock walls. In the dim change room I felt an eerie sensation of standing in a jail cell. I locked the window and ran to open the front door.

Once inside, Ken was all in, seeing the opportunity for uninterrupted basketball time on a full court. We turned on just enough lights to see the baskets. Grabbing balls one by one from the ball rack, we shot baskets until we were drenched in sweat and basketballs were strewn everywhere. We were in basketball heaven. There was no bell to end recess and no competition among the usual crowd of twenty plus kids waiting for a ball to bounce their way.

The plan worked. My shooting and dribbling improved with my extra weekend practice, noted by my coach, until one Monday morning when word came to the principal that the window in the boys' locker room was found open, and a few basketballs were not on the ball rack. We had gotten careless. A general announcement was made to all the classes about the break-in and how it was hoped that no one in the school would do such a thing. Also, a rumor spread that the perpetrator was one of the preacher's kids and that some basketballs had been stolen. The last part was *not* true. We had never taken anything. Naturally, some of my classmates asked me if I'd done it because they wanted to have one of the basketballs I'd supposedly stolen, but I denied being the guy.

"How could I even reach the window without a boost?" I protested. "It's six feet off the ground from the outside, and then I'd have to crawl through. You'd have to be pretty skinny to get through, man, it hardly opens a crack. Plus, the window would have to be unlatched before—"

I stopped, realizing I'd given a few too many details for someone who knew nothing about it. My classmates just stared at me, eager to hear the whole story of how I'd done it. To their credit, they never squealed on me.

My breaking in had one unintended consequence. I had apparently inspired others toward similar activity. The janitor had been kind enough to unlocked the gym first thing in the morning to let us shoot baskets a few minutes before school started. But a few days after my break-in was discovered, one morning we found the gym door locked. For unmentioned reasons, it had been determined the gym would be kept locked during off school hours until further notice.

We were mad. It was a privilege we figured we deserved, and taking it away, we assumed, was mean-spirited and unreasonable. The next morning three guys told me to follow along to the gym. Mark pulled a jackknife from his pocket.

"What are you doing?" I asked.

"Shhh!"

He carefully pushed the knife blade between the door jam and door and gave the knife a slight twist. There was a click, and the door opened. We played basketball until the bell rang for the start of school and then left quietly, making sure the door locked behind us. This went on for a few mornings as the crowd of gym enthusiasts grew, literally riding our shirttails. Then, as with my own previous break-in, word of our adventures spread like grasshoppers through a cornfield in search of lunch.

That was enough. The gavel came down from on high, and an investigation ensued. Principal Bosman's first step was to look for snitches who could shed light on the event. The girls simply shook their heads in unison. "No... Not us... Don't know." Bosman had obviously underestimated our student solidarity. When he failed to find informants, all the junior high boys who had complained about the gym closure were hauled into his office one by one for direct interrogation.

I sat before Mr. Bosman in his office, where once, when I was in fourth grade, he had given me and several guys five swats each for playing out of bounds during recess. He was normally a mild mannered, kind man, who genuinely cared about guiding his charges in the right direction. But he had been criticized for being too soft, so we assumed he was just trying to show how tough he could be. Here I was again. I glanced around his office, at his old wooden desk and out his big window, where a mixture of snow and rain was coming down. Bosman shuffled some papers on his desk and sat back with his small, thin hands folded over his stomach.

"Your dad would not be too proud of you, would he, Karl?" he said, his high-pitched voice crackling.

"About what?"

"Oh, about things of late." He wore an inscrutable smile.

"I suppose not," I said, not knowing what to say.

"Why not, do you suppose?"

"Because I'm no better than anyone else."

"No, I guess not."

I studied the floor. I did not tell him that my dad actually had many occasions not to be too proud of me, far worse than something as trivial as breaking into our school gym. I also didn't tell him that my dad as well as my friends' dads had paid for the gym in the first place, so how could we break into a gym we already owned? It was more like someone forgetting their keys than breaking in. As Mr. Bosman talked, I kept thinking, "Mountain out of a molehill."

"And the window in the locker room?" he suddenly interjected.

I felt my face go hot.

"It's important to tell the truth regardless of the outcome," he said. "Breaking and entering is a crime, you know."

"I didn't do it," I said, offering the half-truth that neither the weekend entries nor the ones before school were actually break-ins, and I wasn't actually the one doing the knife trick. Perjury and obstruction of justice were terms I'd never been exposed to. I didn't offer him anything else. Bosman finally sighed, tired of me and tired of playing cop, it seemed.

But he must have eventually got what he needed out of somebody because one day the four of us who initially got into the gym with Mark's knife trick were being hauled in before our judge and jury, Mr. Bosman, one more time. We stood like a police lineup. I thought we'd be getting five swats again, and it would be over with. Instead, he told us they knew we'd done it and that our punishment would be 500 lines. Writing lines was a standard punishment, but one I hated worse than any other because I wrote so slowly, and it meant being kept in the classroom during recess. "Lines" involved writing a sentence of our teacher's choice over and over, in this case 500 times, until the message was drummed into our heads.

Our line for this offense was, "Breaking and entering is a crime." The other three guys finished quickly, tongues hanging out as they wrote, speeding up when they heard the voices of our classmates having fun outside, but I was still writing lines two days later.

"Stop erasing mistakes and writing so neat," Mark told me. "They don't check it anyway. Here." He showed me how to tape four pencils together to right four lines at once, which I figured cut my time served by a day. Mark was as clever at doing time as he was at using a knife.

Writing those lines was enough to stop me from attempting any more dumb moves at school, but I failed to apply what I'd learned toward responsible behavior in society as a whole. In a few weeks I had developed a penchant for shoplifting. It started simply, with snatching candy. And it wasn't as if I was the only kid who did it, so the offense was easy to minimize. I started by taking the occasional jawbreaker or licorice whip that I could shove easily into my jacket pocket, until I was eventually picking up candy bars by the handful and stuffing them into every available pocket I had. But I didn't make the mistake of one kid who got way too greedy, stuffing so much candy down his jeans that it fell out his pant leg all over the floor as he bolted for the door.

I found two like-minded partners, Evan and Nigel. We worked like wolves in a pack by separating the owner from his goods. While two of us went to the counter to ask the clerk to show us where the kites or baseballs were, the third person would load his pockets with just enough candy that the owner wouldn't notice anything missing. Then we'd go to the park and divide the spoils. We got sick from eating too much, but the thrill of the take was intoxicating.

It was around that time, too, that I tried smoking. Kids picked up smoking like they learned to hunt or drive, in due course. The adults did it, so when we turned twelve or thirteen, we figured it was time we did it too. The only problem was getting our hands on cigarettes. We'd have to beg for them or buy them off someone over eighteen who could buy them at stores. At thirty-five cents a pack they weren't cheap, so we had to pool our resources and share.

Even in the face of new health warnings about smoking, smoke billowed from under the bridge as from a coal burning plant. Below, a crowd of junior high kids were lighting up. My brother Don tried to have a serious talk with me and Ken about smoking to dissuade us from ever starting. He took a long drag on his cigarette and, smoke rising from his mouth and nose, he told us never to start smoking because it was a filthy habit. He then threw his cigarette to the ground and crushed it with his foot. His speech only convinced me I should give it a try.

Under the bridge Evan pulled me aside and took his hand from his coat pocket to show me two full packs of cigarettes.

"Where'd you get those!"

"Follow me and I'll show you," Evan said, grabbing me by the arm.

We walked to the corner gas station near his house. Bill Walston, the owner, was working the station alone. Evan pointed to the shop, where the convenience counter was.

"But how did you buy them without a driver's licence?"

"Buy them? When Wally went out to the pumps to help someone, I just wandered in through the side door and grabbed them," he said casually. "Your turn's next."

"I don't know."

"There's no one else working. He'll never see you. Get us some Salems."

"If I do it, I'll take the kind I want—Marlboros."

"Good enough."

Before I knew it, I'd gone all in. As we spoke, a large truck and trailer pulled up providentially to the pumps with a load of hay six bales high. It would take Wally awhile to fill the customer up with gas, and the hay truck was a perfect shield between the pumps and the convenience desk.

"Man, you are lucky," Evan said. "This one is easy. Go for it."

I followed my feet into the shop through the side door, scarcely conscious that I was moving. My chest pounded. I looked over the convenience desk at the columns of cigarette packs hanging against the wall to locate what I wanted. I heard Wally chatting up the driver at the pumps and glanced out to see two pairs of legs below the level of the trailer with the top half of the two men hidden by the load of hay. I slid behind the counter, reached up, took a pack of Marlboros and one of Salems, and slid back out the door.

Evan caught up to me, grabbing at my pockets.

"Stop," I said. "Wait till we're out of here!"

A light rain started to fall. We put up the hoods of our windbreakers as we walked on casually with our hands in our pockets. We stopped at the Assumptions Church, which was no longer in use, found a crawl space, and pushed through the square opening. Under the church, we lit up, our hearts still pounding with the rush of the heist and the anticipation of our secret indulgence. Our cigarette ends glowed orange in the dark space. I coughed.

"Don't inhale at first," Evan said as if I didn't know anything. "You'll get used to it after awhile."

The lack of ventilation meant we were inhaling some smoke twice. After we'd finished one cigarette, we lit another, and then another. When the taste of tobacco had gone stale and the excitement passed, a heavy sense of guilt came like a gust of wind out of nowhere and settled beneath my ribs. I sat staring up in silence at the underside of the old Assumptions Church.

"It's fantastic." Evan said and laughed.

Without another word, I handed Evan the rest of my cigarettes, crawled back through the square hole to daylight, and squinted at the sky. My mouth and throat felt like dust and tasted cruddy. The rain had stopped, and the sun was trying to break through as I walked slowly home, kicking a stone ahead of me on the way. I never lit up or shoplifted again. I was reformed.

Later in the spring of that same year, 1968, two other crimes of far greater significance occurred, crimes that were not my doing. They made all my wrongdoing look like sandbox play—worse than breaking and entering, stealing smokes, pushing Johnny off the roof, or shooting songbirds—because these two crimes shook the world.

Somewhere far from Sumas, at the other end of the country, someone shot Martin Luther King. Like most white kids my age, I wasn't paying much attention to King or what he was about. But I did see the marches on TV, heard his "I Have A Dream" speech, and knew he was causing a stir. I also knew King was preaching nonviolence and not committing crimes. So when the news came that he'd been gunned down, I was mystified. How could this happen to a good person who was only talking about doing what was good and right?

"Dad, he was a preacher, like you," I said.

"Yes, a Baptist preacher."

"Are you afraid of being shot?"

Dad just looked at me.

"Did he have any kids?" I asked.

"A couple, I believe."

That was all I ever heard my dad say about King. He didn't mention his name from the pulpit or in conversations with parishioners. The best I could gather was that he was either embarrassed by it or as puzzled as I was.

Bobby Kennedy was running for president that year. He was the only politician who ever grabbed my interest in any way to that point. Politicians, I'd noticed, usually served up a lot of cheese, but Bobby sounded genuine. I was attracted to his soft-spoken, youthful manner. He seemed to care about people and understand people's suffering. The day Martin Luther King was killed, Bobby stopped his campaign to tell his audience what had just happened. He told them he understood the King family's grief because of how he'd lost his brother Jack.

Two months later while Kennedy was campaigning in California, I was watching the news with my dad. Kennedy's support was growing, and it looked like he might be the one to represent the Democratic Party.

"Do you think he'll be president," I asked Dad.

"He might very well be. He's smart and attractive enough."

It was rare for my dad, a die-hard republican, to speak positively about a democrat. Even he was impressed with Bobby.

"If Bobby Kennedy wins," I said, "does that mean the war is going to be over?"

"That's what he says."

"Then Dale won't go to Vietnam?"

"Maybe not."

Kennedy had just finished a speech and was walking away from the podium when, suddenly, screaming and confusion broke out. The news reporter announced, "Senator Kennedy has been shot . . . he is down . . . there is blood . . ." His wife was leaning over him on the floor in the pandemonium. A few hours later Bobby Kennedy was dead.

I was angry after that. I asked Dad why people hated the Kennedys so much.

"I don't know," he said. "There are a lot of bad people in the world."

No one could explain two assassinations of two good people in two months' time. After JFK, King, and Bobby, I was sure that anyone who wanted to be a leader and a voice for good would become the target of a gun. What was wrong with these killers? How did they ever get started shooting people? I felt sick wondering if they had ever shot birds, like I had, or ever shoplifted, or broken into places.

After Bobby Kennedy was killed, everybody thought Nixon was a shoo-in to be the next president. Bumper stickers all over town declared "Nixon's the One." And he did win in the end. He promised peace, but he didn't seem like the type who was interested in ending the war. Strangely, no one I knew seemed to care, maybe because the shooting and killing had been going on for so long—so much death, everywhere.

— Chapter 20 —

Gathering

Mom was on cloud nine. All her chicks were coming home for Christmas. 1968 had been a sad and tragic year for America, and gathering for Christmas felt like the right thing to do.

Sharon arrived from Michigan, newly married to John, an affable and communicative guy if you liked talking about politics or guns. He didn't bring his guns, but he came with a loaded camera strapped around his neck. He wore the camera constantly, keeping it propped on a generous stomach. You never knew when you'd become the next candid portrait in his collection. Dale was on a break from flight training and would be off to Vietnam sometime in the new year. Nancy was coming home from an anxious semester after her first year in college. Shirley was delighted to be on an extended break from boarding school.

Don arrived last from Washington DC, where he'd just finished Navy duty. He brought with him his new girlfriend from the big city, Georgine, a breath of fresh air. Her coming was big news with Mom, who was overly nice trying to make our family seem respectable. Georgine was different, well mannered and carefully groomed, a real show stopper. Mom was delighted having someone in the house who cared about how they looked and behaved. And Georgine must have had a pretty good hold on Don. He was clucking around the house like a rooster, cooing nonsensically, and planting kisses on her in the middle of the living room. It was weird seeing him so unabashedly romantic. Where had my brother gone?

Ken, Keith, and I watched as they all trickled in, bringing tales and pickings from far off lands, places I and my two young brothers were destined for one day also—colleges, careers, military, the unknown—dispersed into the wild and unpredictable world. Their arrival filled up every square foot of space in the house and raised the decibel level to an even ten.

New stories converged with old stories as everyone competed over the best tales, voices rising in a crescendo around the supper table. One person's story tumbled over that of another like Christmas parcels being unloaded and thrown under the tree. We were used to having to try hard to be heard. Sharon, Don, and Dale, the three oldest in the family, were the loudest although Shirley asserted herself quite well when she wanted to. "The Three K's" created our own pandemonium. Even Nancy in the middle, the quietest and gentlest among us, could bring the volume up when she needed to.

"These drivers on the West Coast," Don was saying, "don't know how to handle a little snow. If you drove like that in DC—"

"Oh, yeah," Sharon laughed, "I've seen how you handle it."

"Mom, when should we make the cider?"

"What's that? Make what higher?"

"Why don't you have your Christmas tree up yet, Dad?"

"We were waiting for you guys so one of you could pick one up."

Meanwhile, Sharon's John turned circles, trying to find familiarity in this foreign land. Ah, there was Sharon now. Georgine shook her head in bewilderment. Any outsider would find the cacophony more than a bit unnerving. I had to give the newcomers credit for trying to fit in.

"After my first date with your sister," John said. "it was all over. I knew I had her."

Sharon chuckled. We waited for her side of the story, but that was it.

Our collection of Christmas vinyls played nonstop—Perry Como, Bing Crosby, Frank Sinatra, Andy Williams, Glen Campbell, Doris Day, Johnny Cash, and Mom's sacred music groups who sang "real Christmas carols." We would have to replace the needle on the turntable before the holidays were over.

Mom, trying to get our attention, finally yelled sharply over the din, "Hey!" Everyone like chickens in a coop went suddenly quiet and looked her way, which cracked Mom up. She was happy whatever the decibel level—she had her family home.

"What I've been trying to say," Mom said, "does anyone want *oliebollen*?" They were literally "oil balls," blobs of dough dropped in hot oil that came out looking like lumpy donut holes, a standard Dutch Christmas treat, also coated with sugar to intensify the cardiovascular effects. Another guilty Christmas pleasure was *banket*, almond paste rolled up in flakey pastry dough, which was equally damaging. Either treat could induce a winter coma after only a few bites.

On the fireplace mantel sat our favorite Christmas knickknack because it involved fire—angels on a carousel ringing bells as they hovered above lit candles, which prompted the celestial beings to stay busy. They turned perpetually in circles as long as the candles didn't go out. On the living room floor in front of the big picture window, sat the metal tree stand, waiting for a Christmas tree. Next to it sat boxes of our never-changing ornaments ready to go up on the not-yet-there tree. Don said he had a plan for a tree, which he wasn't sharing at the moment. Dad had the lights strung up outside, arranged the same way every year, to greet the family as they rolled in. On the roof he perched his large star cut out of a sheet of plywood. It had holes for lights, the only one of its kind. Dad was quite proud of it even though he had to climb up to set it straight a couple times after a stiff wind coming down the Fraser Valley sent it off-kilter. These were the reminders that in a world of change there was firm ground and comfort in Christmas.

Don taught us how to play Pinochle that Christmas, something he'd picked up in the Navy. Pinochle and board games occupied one card table and jigsaw puzzles another throughout the holiday. Mom wasn't fond of cards entering the house though because it looked too much like gambling. She would have much preferred us playing games with traditional American values, like Monopoly.

"It's not gambling, Mom. What would we gamble with?"

"Well . . . money, which we don't have."

A couple of days before Christmas, Dad and Mom let us each open one small gift to accommodate our rising anxiety. Ken and I opened plastic models of army helicopters, a Huey and a Cobra. We had to show Dale.

"Is this what you're going to fly in Vietnam?" I asked.

"No," Dale explained patiently, "those are attack helicopters. I'll be flying bigger ones, Chinooks. They're for transport not attacks. My chopper's got two rotors and looks like an eggbeater upside down, like this." He held his hands with his fingers pointing up like rotors.

"How do you fly it?"

"Two peddles and two sticks, one stick on the side and one in front of you."

"Sounds like a bike!"

"Yeah, almost. You just give 'er some throttle and pull up on the stick at your side, like this." He demonstrated with imaginary controls. "And when you get that baby off the ground, you tilt forward a little bit on the stick in front of you like this . . . " He sucked in some drool at the corner of his mouth. "And whoosh, off she goes."

"And what about shooting?" Ken asked. "You have to shoot, don't you?"

"Not me, I'm busy flying. We have mounted guns, but other guys in the crew take care of that if we come under fire. My job is to keep us out of trouble so we don't end up like that there." He pointed to our model helicopter parts scattered over the floor.

"You won't," Ken said confidently.

Families' lives had been changed forever by Vietnam, but no one, not even Mom and Dad, talked to us about the dangers of what Dale was going into, for our protection. The grim realities of war were kept hidden under the twin blankets of blind duty and a naive sense that all would be well.

That winter we were plunged into a cold snap howling down the Fraser Valley from the interior. The roads were ploughed to an icy sheen. Sledding on Mose Hill Road was at a prime. In the back of the garage we found our sleds, wood slats on metal frames. With the sun sinking around mid afternoon, the road was growing especially icy, which gave us good speed all afternoon. Nancy was a maniac. She got a running start stomach first and picked up speed all the way to the flat, where we saw her shrunk to the size of a dot in the distance, shooting out of sight across the railroad tracks. She appeared again, "joy to the world" writ bold as she waved up jubilantly. She warned us it was getting too slick. The sun was setting, and gruesome tales of sledding accidents convinced us we should probably wrap it up. We made our way back to the house, cold and craving *oliebollen*.

The next day, Christmas Eve, we got up early to make the most of the heavy snowfall. Ken, Keith, and I created networks of tunnels in the snowdrifts. Mom poured us some hot apple cider, which we could drink in our central snow room "like Eskimos" as steam filled our small domed space.

Don and Georgine emerged from the house with Shirley on their heels. They called for us to join them for an outing to the woods. Don threw a handsaw, a roll of twine, and a plastic sheet into the trunk, and we clambered into the car.

"What's all that stuff for?" Keith asked.

"You'll find out when we get up into the hills."

I sat in the front seat next to Georgine, who shoved over against Don. Shirley, Ken and Keith sat in the back.

"We gonna kill somebody?" I said.

"Yep, and then cut them into pieces and wrap them in plastic."

Shirley shouted, "Don't do it, Don!"

Georgine jabbed him in the ribs while everyone screamed that they didn't want to go. As we neared the mountains, he tried to explain the lay of the land to Georgine, who was seeing it all for the first time.

"I love it," she said.

She seemed to love it even more because of who else loved it. Don pointed out his favorite and least favorite features of the area.

"I like how the mountains jut straight up from the valley," Georgine said.

"Once you're in those foothills, you just climb and climb, and there's nothing but virgin forest after that."

"What's virgin?" Keith asked.

Georgine grinned, keeping her carefully groomed head facing straight ahead, waiting for Don to explain.

"It means unspoiled by man," Don said.

Georgine coughed. "By *man*," she repeated

"Lookit here," Don said. "Somebody cleared this area right along the river for no good reason. Shoot, that'll just erode and choke out all the fish. Don't anyone blame me when you come here next time and can't fish anymore."

"Okay, we've been warned, and we won't blame you," Georgine said and tickled him.

Don flinched. "Hey, don't, I'm trying to drive here."

"Hey, he's trying to drive here, Georgine!" Shirley laughed and clapped in appreciation of their banter, and then added a big "Yee! Haw!"

We wound our way up a gravel road until we reached the Kamphouse farm about a mile into the hills.

"Why are we stopping here?" I asked as Don got out.

Mr. Kamphouse directed Don up a lane that led into a wooded area on his property. "You'll find a pasture up there, about five acres." He handed Don a long two-man saw, with a handle at each end. "You might need this. You can take anything you find in the woods around that clearing, big or small, doesn't matter."

Don said the saw was probably more than we needed but thanked him and threw it into the trunk. Farther up, at the end of a dirt lane, we parked and stepped out, where Don finally explained why we'd come. We were looking for a good Christmas tree. It was a romantic notion, going off into the bush to cut our own tree. We'd be doing it the natural way, not settling for one of those plastic trees you can get at the hardware store. What fun would that be? We also shunned the cultivated varieties that they planted on reclaimed marshland in unnatural rows, then cut, and lined up against the wall of the grocery store.

"Okay, let's spread out a little into the woods but stay within shouting distance," Don explained.

"No shouting, Don!" Shirley said.

"Quiet, Shirley, too loud," he said. "Everybody stay close to the edge of the clearing. Look for a tree that's maybe a bit taller than I am."

"Taller like Georgine?" Shirley said, and we all laughed. "Yee, hee!"

Every few seconds someone thought they'd found a good Christmas tree, and we all came running to throw in our two bits of evaluation. Most trees we found were thin and scrawny.

"I got one," I heard Keith say. He stood with his head cocked, curiously considering a short scruffy tree as if it were a new kid on the block that for all its flaws he found kind of interesting.

"See this?" Don pointed to a Douglas fir. "That's the kind we want."

"Why not this one?" Keith asked.

"Because firs make the best Christmas trees, and there's more of them, so nobody's going to miss one little tree if we take one out."

It was tough to find a tree of the right size, perfect shape, and right kind. With Christmas Eve fading, this was our last chance to get a tree, and we thought we'd be coming home empty handed. Don was getting miffed. Here he'd taken Georgine out in the woods for a Kit Carson experience, and the woods were threatening to show him up right in front his girlfriend.

"Did Mr. Kamphouse say we could take down any tree?" I asked, "because there's a perfect Christmas tree right up there." I pointed to the top of a fifty-foot Douglas fir. Everyone liked the look of it from where we stood.

"Who's gonna climb up there and get it?" Ken said.

"Climb up there!" Shirley shouted. "Come on, Karl, do it!"

We glanced around at other trees. Don finally conceded. "Okay, let's take it down."

"The whole thing?" someone asked.

"Yep."

We gazed up at the winning candidate. It was an extreme ambition to be cutting down the whole tree just for the bit at the top. But the crown looked perfect, and by this time no one was in an arguing mood. It would be good for the forest, Don said, just a modest thinning, and Mr. Kamphouse would thank us for clearing a little more of his land for pasture.

The tree was around two feet in diameter. We were going to need the two-man saw after all. Don ran back to the car and returned with the saw, looking regretful about our mission. Kneeling at the base of the tree, he and I grabbed a handle each. We'd make a cut on one side of the tree, he said, and then a cut on the opposite side a bit higher, and let the tree fall into the clearing.

"I don't want you to get killed," Don said as we started. "When the tree starts going, back away. These things can buck like a bronco."

We quickly caught the rhythm of the two-handled saw, but we noticed immediately getting through the tree would require endurance. We paused for a breather. The noble warrior was refusing to go down. It had won my respect, which made taking it down all the more difficult. Finally, there was a slight lean to the tree.

"It's going, back away," Don said and gave the trunk a push. It leaned, Don fell back, and the tree fell in slow motion into the clearing, landing with a muffled thud. We cut off the top six feet and held it up like conquerors displaying the head of the enemy. There were forced cheers and tepid applause. Up close the tree did not look as full as it had looked from fifty feet below. It was actually quite spindly. A mix of guilt and resignation settled in.

"Well, Kamphouse has a little more pasture now, and he can use the rest of the tree for firewood," Don said, trying to put a positive spin on our work.

Above the clearing the sky was turning a steely blue as the sun set beyond the trees. The first star was out. A damp chill filled the spaces between us. The felling of the tree, lopping of its top, and carrying it away evoked silent protest from somewhere in the universe, piercing our gathering with a twinge of unspoken regret—silent night, holy night.

Don and I silently carried the six-foot treetop between us like a bier on which our transgressions lay. At the car, Don stepped awkwardly over an icy patch and groaned, clutching his back. We pushed the tree into the trunk, bending it slightly at the tip to fit it in. Everyone was tired on the ride home. The only sound was an occasionally groan from Don as he grabbed at his back, and all of us were thinking the same thing—the fallen warrior had gotten in a final blow.

We set up our tree using Dad's vintage metal stand, placing it in front of the large picture window, where it looked out sadly toward the hills from whence it came. Dad stared at it skeptically.

"Whereja get it?"

"Kamphouses," Don said before anyone else tried to tell the full story. Dad might not approve of occupying the house with such an extreme sacrifice. The story was better left untold until perhaps next Christmas around the dinner table.

Once Dale and Don had strung the lights on the tree, everyone grabbed their favorite ornaments to put up. Sharon and Nancy strictly forbade anyone from tossing the tinsel icicles onto the tree. They were to be put on as gently as an evening snow fall. The presents came last, placed under the tree with the tags hidden to keep their givers and recipients as concealed as possible. But Ken, Keith, and I lay prone before the tree anyway, trying to read the tags.

"You don't have to worship the tree," John quipped.

"We're not, we're worshipping the presents," Keith said.

That night we turned on the TV to see what was happening with Apollo 8, which registered large on my radar. The mission was a warm up for a moon landing coming sometime next year. After a year of fear and sadness, NASA thought it would be good for people to lift their eyes to the heavens, and the timing could not have been better. The spacecraft with her three astronauts had entered the moon's orbit. We leaned forward as pictures of the moon's surface were being sent back to earth. The far side of the moon, which no one had ever seen, came into view, barren and mysterious. Then, as the spaceship rounded the far side, we saw earth rise on the moon's horizon—a misty blue half circle in a vast sea of blackness, so fragile, so insignificant it startled us. There we sat, looking at ourselves from God's view.

"That's where we live?" Keith said. His astonishment spoke for all of us.

Then, as if on cue, the astronauts began reading from the book of Genesis. "In the beginning, God created the heavens and the earth . . . " The timing of the message on Christmas Eve could hardly be lost on anyone. The earth, a speck in the universe, was important enough to be inhabited by God and claimed as his home.

Before signing off, the Apollo 8 commander quipped, "Please be informed, there *is* a Santa Claus," and we all howled.

When it came to Santa and the material side of Christmas, we got more excited than you'd expect as preacher's kids, while Dad was trying to put together a meaningful Christmas message about the one from heaven born into poverty on our tiny planet. Ken, Keith, and I were consumed with Rock 'em Sock 'em Robots and Monopoly while Jesus was laying it all out on the line in a cold barn. But it was nearly impossible to convince any kid, even if his dad was a pastor, that presents were not the highlight of Christmas.

The real meaning of Christmas had to fight its way through my thick skull. I was obsessed with finding where Mom hid the presents before she got around to wrapping them. I discovered them above the washer and dryer, behind the detergent, and showed Ken. If we noticed a gift on the shelf we didn't like, we'd drop a hint such as "I sure would never want you to waste your money on an Etch A Sketch for Christmas" in hopes that the Etch A Sketch might get returned before being put under the tree.

My parents knew they couldn't beat the materialism of the season, so they would at least try to make it palatable. They would accommodate it somehow. To drive a theological point home, Dad and Mom said we would open our presents only *after* the Christmas service. We would receive the Christ of Christmas first and the material blessings second, as a bonus rather than an entitlement.

My parents didn't rail against Santa like some people did. Some stopped Santa at the door along with the Christmas tree. But our parents more or less took Santa in as a guest, flawed and doctrinally unenlightened as he was, accepting him as a reflection of our human vices as well as a chance to put things into perspective. Like Santa, none of us were perfect. There was room in Christmas for everyone, most of all room for characters like Santa.

That said, Mom or Dad never tried to fool us into thinking an omnipresent Santa Claus miraculously delivered us our presents under the tree each year. My parents retained the privilege of gift giving for their own good pleasure, a joy they would never forfeit to a fantasy in a red and white suit with flying escorts. They paid him his respects, like paying taxes to Caesar, but they would not let him turn the house into a den of extortion and bribery on the holiest of days. The pleasure of giving belonged to them and God.

As Ken and I peered under the tree, I recognized immediately the box that must have contained the Aurora race car set we had asked for. It was the most elaborate setup available from the Sears catalogue, designed with a corkscrew, a long straightaway, a banked curve, two cars, and trigger controls. I knew we had to have it the moment I saw it. I lost sleep imagining the control in my hand, racing against Ken. I became the driver in the car, spinning sideways through corners and roaring through the checkered flag.

But there had been a problem. At thirty dollars, the race car set was way over my parents' limit of ten dollars per person they would spend. In a family of eight kids the Christmas budget added up fast, a stretch for my parents, especially when adding gifts for people outside the family. We knew arguments with Dad about money were always fruitless, so we didn't normally try to negotiate.

But with the electric race car set of my dreams on the horizon, these were not normal times. First I had to convince Ken to go in with me as partners on the racing set and see if we could negotiate an acquisition from our parents. It was a long shot, but Ken was keen on the idea. We pooled five dollars from our own pockets and added that amount to our designated ten dollars each for a total of twenty-five dollars. We would ask Mom and Dad to match our personal contribution with an extra five dollars of their own to make the full thirty. It seemed fair and reasonable enough. We took our pitch to Mom, thinking she'd be the easiest sell.

Holding the catalogue up in front of her, Ken put a finger on the large color photo of the Aurora corkscrew track and looked straight into Mom's eyes while I gave my best sales pitch. "Do you think your boys would like to have this for a Christmas they'd never forget for their entire lives? You could shop for just this one item instead of two, it's easy. Just look at these curves." I traced my finger over the track in the photo.

Mom snickered. I added, "As a bonus, we'll put in five dollars of our own money, and that way you'd only need to add an extra five to make this the best Christmas ever."

"Thirty dollars is a lot of money for a present," she said more to herself than to us. I knew the hook was set when she said she'd take the catalogue for a second opinion.

"It sounds okay to me," she told Dad as he lifted his head briefly from his sermon preparation.

Dad was not as impressed with the race car set as he was with our business acumen. How we'd thought of financing the gift evoked a sense of pride, and not having to think about what to get us, and being able to get it in one stop were all strong selling points. He was in and Ken and I were elated looking forward to the best Christmas ever.

Dad's Christmas sermon gave the congregation something to stew over for the holidays. As he concluded, he said, "Jesus was born to give his life for the whole world, not only for those of us sitting here, so spread the good news." He left it at that without any qualifications, such as how this was only true "for those God chose as his elect people." Some mysteries were best left without trying to explain them. A couple of elders later had to challenge him on his proposition, as expected, with questions about predestination. Dad didn't waver and added to his original statement, "Not only is Jesus God's gift to the world, but so is the question he poses: 'Who will receive it?'" I liked how Dad said what he believed and rarely backed down from what he said even if others didn't always agree.

Christmas night, after the church service, our family bacchanalia erupted with the usual tsunami of red and green paper and ribbons flooding the living room, everyone awash in gifts and apple cider. Eggnog and *oliebollen* rolled down our gullets, our hands dove into bowls of party mix, and jokes ebbed and flowed while Bing Crosby sang "I'll Be Home for Christmas."

Ken and I spent every spare minute the following days setting up our race track and jumping on the controls, racing nonstop. Arguments inevitably erupted when a car got nudged off the track on a curve or when we had a tight finish. We did reach the point of exhaustion, accompanied by a mysterious sense of sadness, realizing how not even the race car set could bring endless satisfaction. We put the controls down and left the track before going back to it again a few days later.

The high of Christmas turned like a hinge on the back door as siblings began to leave again to far off places. Sharon and John returned to Detroit, where Sharon was starting her career in nursing. Nancy flew back for another semester of college, and we drove Shirley back to boarding school. Dale hung around as long as he could before jumping back into flight training, preparing to deploy to Nam. If he was worried about getting killed, he didn't show it.

Don saw Georgine off at the airport, back to DC, sensing somehow their relationship would not last. After sharing our family Christmas, had they realized their ways and manners didn't mesh? Something just wasn't right about it, Don said.

Regardless of our imperfections, our arguments, or the paths we chose, our coming together at Christmas was a sign of what lasted. The same ornaments were hung on the tree, the same carols were sung, and the same message was heard. And if we happened to forget, Christmas always presented us with the same question—"Who will receive it?"

Long after everyone had left, our tree still stood in the picture window, alone, sparse, twiggy, and natural. We had culled it from the woods for what we deemed the greater good, which was our Christmas pleasure. On the top branch the star perched, looking a little beat up over the years, its silver paint chipped and cracked. No matter how hard we had tried to stand it up straight, the star kept bowing. Its center was a series of concentric circles, a weary, longsuffering eye looking down, as if it understood this family of comers and goers with all our charms and flaws.

Acknowledgements

THANK YOU, FIRST AND foremost, to my family, who read many of the chapters in this collection and offered their opinions, arguments, praise, and suggestions. They have sharpened my memory and softened my biases. This book would obviously not be my story without them. I apologize if I have not included all their ideas and perspectives. There could be at least seven other books among us that would add to our collective experiences. And how do I properly thank my parents, whose love and devotion to each other, family, and God literally brought my story into being?

Thank you to Carolyn Scriven for pointing out the weaknesses in my manuscript and for lauding its strengths. I'm deeply humbled and indebted to her for her selfless, critical attention to my work. I am deeply grateful for the services of someone so experienced.

Thanks also to my patient, expeditious editor, Lydia Forssander-Song, for making sense of my odd colloquialisms, and for prodding at my lines and paragraphs to help them make sense.

I am grateful to my friends for their support in this writing adventure even when they couldn't understand what I was up to. Especially, thank you to Corey Porter for the hours he devoted to reading my manuscript and offering valuable feedback while asking nothing in return. Thanks again to my faithful reader and critic, Nikki Winter, who quickly felt the pulse of the story and found the places where it skipped a beat.

I would like to acknowledge Kwantlen Polytechnic University for their partial funding of this project.

Finally, thank you, Diane, my wife, for giving me the title for this book and for taking on extra home duties to allow me to bring it to completion. You are amazing.

www.ingramcontent.com/pod-product-compliance
Lightning Source LLC
Chambersburg PA
CBHW072137160426
43197CB00012B/2137